# *UGC NET/SET DI EST MARKETING MANAGEMENT*

AF517083

Book Title: UGC NET/SET DIGEST MARKETING MANAGEMENT
Book Author: Dr.Aasim Mir
Published by: SMART MOVES PUBLICATION
E-5/11 Above Woodland Showroom, Bitten Market
Bhopal -462038 (M.P.) India.

Printed and bound by: SMART MOVES PUBLICATION
E-5/11 Above Woodland Showroom, Bitten Market
Bhopal -462038 (M.P.) India.

This edition published in: 2019 ISBN (ISBN Pending)
Copyright ©2019 by Dr.Aasim Mir
Dr.Aasim Mir asserts the moral right to be identified as the author of this work.
9788193593097
This book is a work of fiction and any resemblance to actual persons, living or dead, events and locales is purely coincidental.

All rights reserved. No part of this publication may be reproduced, stored in or introduced into a retrieval system, or transmitted, in any form, or by any means (electrical, mechanical, photocopying, recording or otherwise) without the prior written permission of the author or publisher. Any person who does any unauthorised act in relation to this publication may be liable to criminal prosecution and civil claims for damages.

SMART MOVES
India. USA.
ISBN xxx-x-xxxxx-xx-x

This book has been published with all reasonable efforts taken to make the material error-free after the consent of the author. No part of this book shall be used, reproduced in any manner whatsoever without written permission from the publisher, except in the case of brief quotations embodied in critical articles and reviews.

The Author of this book is solely responsible and liable for its content including but not limited to the views, representations, descriptions, statements, information, opinions and references ["Content"]. The Content of this book shall not constitute or be construed or deemed to reflect the opinion or expression of the Publisher or Editor. Neither the Publisher nor Editor endorse or approve the Content of this book or guarantee the reliability, accuracy or completeness of the Content published herein and do not make any representations or warranties of any kind, express or implied, including but not limited to the implied warranties of merchantability, fitness for a particular purpose. The Publisher and Editor shall not be liable whatsoever for any errors, omissions, whether such errors or omissions result from negligence, accident, or any other cause or claims for loss or damages of any kind, including without limitation, indirect or consequential loss or damage arising out of use, inability to use, or about the reliability, accuracy or sufficiency of the information contained in this book.

# Preface

Marketing Management is one of the most fundamental areas of concern in this contemporary world. No doubt the phenomenon of designing, manufacturing, estimating benefits and costs have changed a lot but marketing is the functional area that has witnessed crucial level of competition in the recent business arena. It is also one among the most relevant field for research and study for students, scholars as well as other researchers. This book is one such initiative that is equipped with MCQ's on Marketing Management and surely shall help the learners up to greater extent in getting latest knowledge and qualifying competitive examination. The book has been written with one prime objective of providing comprehensive knowledge to those students who are eager to qualify UGC NET/SET/SLET and want to join the prestigious teaching profession. The themes on whom various MCQ's have been covered in this book include understanding of Marketing Management, Marketing Strategies, plans and policies, Corporate and Business level planning, Analyzing Marketing Comprehensions, Internal and external environment and environmental sectors, marketing research and forecasting, customer value analysis, customer and business markets, buying and decision process, segmentation and positioning, building brands, analysis of market competition, product and pricing strategy, designing and management of services, designing of marketing channels, ebusiness and ecommerce, integrated and holistic marketing, promotion mix, global marketing, holistic market orientation, social responsibility and marketing etc.

I hope that the book will be highly appreciated by students, scholars and teachers. Moreover, I welcome all suggestions that will help in appraising contents and enrichment of this book.

**Dr.Aasim Mir**

# MCQ's/Objective Type Questions

1. Marketing is
a) Meeting needs Profitability
b) Planning
c) Execution
d) Profitability
2. In which of the following type of demand consumers dislike products and even pay a price to avoid it.
a) Latent demand
b) Irregular demand
c) Declining demand
d) Negative demand
3. In which of the following type of demand consumers are unaware or uninterested in the product.
a) Negative demand
b) Nonexistent demand
c) Latent demand
d) Full demand
4. Which of the following represents demand based on seasonal pattern

a) Irregular demand
b) Unwholesome demand
c) Nonexistent demand

d) Overfull demand

5. In which type of demand consumers may be attracted to a product having undesirable social consequences.

a) Overfull demand

b) Unwholesome demand

c) Declining demand

d) Negative demand

6. "Information Age" has been a component of

a) Digital Revolution

b) Changing technology

c) Globalization

d) Deregulation

7. The production of individually differentiated goods is called

a) Privatization

b) Industry Convergence

c) Customization

d) Globalization

8. "Brick and Click" falls under

a) Disintermediation

b) Customization

c) Retail Transformation

d) None of these

9. Consumers prefer products that are widely available and inexpensive is an example of

a) Production concept

b) Product Concept

c) Selling concept

d) Marketing concept

10. Consumers shall prefer products having high quality, performance or innovative features falls under

a) Production concept

b) Product concept

c) Selling concept
d) None of these
11. The selling concept is epitomized in the thinking of
a) Philip Kotler
b) Sergio Zyman
c) Chin-Tiong Tan
d) Jacob Hornick
12. Marketing concept emerged in
a) Mid 1950's
b) 1960's
c) Mid 1940's
d) 1970's
. Sense and Respond is a philosophy of<
a) Production concept
b) Marketing concept
c) Selling concept
d) Societal Marketing concept
14. Proactive marketing orientation is associated with
a) Narver and Colleagues
b) Hornick and Associates
c) Zyman and Colleagues
d) None of these
15. Everything matters is linked with
a) Societal marketing
b) Relationship marketing
c) Holistic marketing
d) Internal marketing
16. "They spend time meeting customers and listening to their problems" comes under the preview of
a) R&D
b) Manufacturing
c) Sales

d) Logistics

17. They proactively search for the best suppliers:

a) Manufacturing

b) Marketing

c) Public Relations

d) Purchasing

18. They meet customer requirements for customization where possible:

a) Public Relations

b) Logistics

c) Marketing

d) Manufacturing

19. Which of the following continuously gather and evaluate ideas for new products and services

a) Sales

b) Marketing

c) Public Relations

d) R&D

20. They have specialized knowledge of customer's industry

a) Marketing

b) Sales

c) R&D

d) Public Relations

21. They set a high standard for service delivery time and meet this standard consistently:

a) Sales

b) Marketing

c) Public Relations

d) Logistics

22. They strive to give the customer "The Best Solution"

a) Sales

b) Marketing

c) Manufacturing
d) None of these
23. They tailor the financial package to the customer's financial requirements
a) Budget
b) Finance
c) Marketing
d) Sales
24. Which of the following act as internal customer:
a) Marketing
b) Sales man
c) Public Relation
d) Advertisement
25. Which of the following is responsible for " Supporting behavior change campaigns"
a) Corporate social marketing
b) Cause marketing
c) Cause related marketing
d) Corporate philanthropy
26. Promoting social issues through efforts such as sponsorships, licensing, agreements and advertising falls under the preview of:
a) Corporate social marketing
b) Cause marketing
c) Cause related marketing
d) Corporate philanthropy
27. Donating a percentage of revenue to a specific cause based on the revenue occurring during the announced period of support is called
a) Corporate social marketing
b) Cause marketing
c) Cause related marketing
d) Corporate philanthropy
28. Corporate Philanthropy describes:

a) Supportive behavior change campaign
b) Promoting social issues
c) Providing volunteer services
d) Making gifts to help nonprofit organizations or groups

29. Corporate community involvement accounts for:
a) Supportive behavior change campaign
b) Promoting social issues
c) Providing volunteer services
d) Making gifts to help nonprofit organizations or groups

30. Socially responsible business practices holds:
a) Conducting business practices that protect environment and human rights
b) Supportive behavior change campaign
c) Promoting social issues
d) None of these

31. The need in which a customer wants an inexpensive car is:
a) Stated need
b) Real need
c) Unstated need
d) Delight need

32. The need in which a customer wants a car whose operating cost, not its initial price is low is:
a) Stated need
b) Real need
c) Unstated need
d) Secret need

33. The need in which the customer expects good service from dealer is :
a) Stated need
b) Real need
c) Unstated need
d) Secret need

34. The customer wants that the dealer must include an onboard navigation system is :
a) Stated need
b) Real need
c) Unstated need
d) Delight need
35. The need in which customer wants to be seen as a savvy consumer by friends is:
a) Stated need
b) Real need
c) Unstated need
d) Secret need
36. A value represents:
a) Perceived tangible and intangible benefits.
b) Perceived tangible and intangible benefits and costs to consumers.
c) Perceived tangible benefits.
d) Perceived intangible benefits and costs to consumers.
37. To reach a target market, the marketer uses _________ kinds of marketing channels.
a) One
b) Two
c) Three
d) Four
38. _________type of communication channels deliver and receive messages from target buyers and include newspapers, magazines etc.
a) Communication Channels
b) Distribution Channels
c) Service Channels
d) Both a & b
39. In which of the following type of channels, the marketer uses to display, sell or deliver the physical product or service to the buyer.
a) Communication Channels

b) Distribution Channels
c) Service Channels
d) Both a & b

40. Which of the following channels are used for carrying out transactions with potential buyers?
a) Communication Channels
b) Distribution Channels
c) Service Channels
d) None of these

41. Which of the following environment includes immediate factors involved in producing, distributing and promoting the offerings?
a) Task Environment
b) Broad Environment
c) International Environment
d) Cultural Environment

42. The first step in marketing planning process is:
a) Selecting target market
b) Analyzing marketing opportunities
c) Designing marketing strategies
d) Developing marketing programs

43. The second step in marketing planning process is:
a) Selecting target market
b) Analyzing marketing opportunities
c) Designing marketing strategies
d) Developing marketing programs

44. The third step in marketing planning process is:
a) Selecting target market
b) Analyzing marketing opportunities
c) Designing marketing strategies
d) Developing marketing programs

45. The fourth step in marketing planning process is:
a) Selecting target market

b) Analyzing marketing opportunities
c) Designing marketing strategies
d) Developing marketing programs
46. The fifth step in marketing planning process is:
a) Selecting target market
b) Analyzing marketing opportunities
c) Managing marketing efforts
d) Developing marketing programs
47. "Marketing is far too important to leave to the marketing department" was said by:
a) David Packard
b) Dennis Riche
c) Jacob Jacoby
d) Carol Berning
48. In case of "Developing Marketing Strategies and Plans" a firm has to:
a) Identify its potential long term opportunities
b) Analyze the happenings inside the firm
c) Analyze the happenings outside the firm
d) Redesign its marketing programs
49. In case of "Capturing Marketing Insights" a firm has to:
a) Understand the happenings inside the firm
b) Understand the happenings outside the firm
c) Understand the happenings both inside and outside the firm
d) Choose a different target market.
50. In case of cross selling a marketer:
a) Sells an old product to a new customer
b) Sells an additional product to existing customer
c) Enters a new market with old product
d) Introduces a new product in old market
51. In case of up selling a marketer:
a) Asks customers to increase volume of sale

b) encourages customers to purchase a comparable higher-end product than the one under consideration

c) Both a and b

d) None of the above

52. The value creation and delivery sequence process consists of:

a) Three Parts

b) Four Parts

c) Five Parts

d) Seven Parts

53. In case of value creation and delivery sequence process second phase is to:

a) Choose the value

b) Communicate the value

c) Provide the value

d) Deliver the value

54. In case of value creation and delivery sequence process third phase is to:

a) Choose the value

b) Communicate the value

c) Provide the value

d) Deliver the value

55. The value creation and delivery sequence process involves:

a) Strategic Marketing

b) Tactical Marketing

c) Relationship Marketing

d) Both a & b

56. Value positioning is the ______ step in "Choose the value" under value creation and delivery sequence process.

a) First

b) Second

c) Third

d) Fourth

57. Service development is the ________ step in "Provide the Value" under value creation and delivery sequence process.

a) First

b) Second

c) Third

d) Fourth

58. Sales promotion is the ________ step in "Communicate the Value" under value creation and delivery sequence process.

a) First

b) Second

c) Third

d) Fourth

59. Pricing is the ________ step in "Provide the Value" under value creation and delivery sequence process.

a) First

b) Second

c) Third

d) Fourth

60. Customer segmentation is the ______ step in "Choose the value" under value creation and delivery sequence process.

a) First

b) Second

c) Third

d) Fourth

61. "Customer feedback should be collected continuously after purchase to learn how to improve the product and its marketing" is called:

a) Zero customer feedback time

b) Zero product improvement time

c) Zero setup time

d) Zero purchasing time

62. "The company should introduce most valued and feasible improvements as soon as possible" is called:

a) Zero customer feedback time

b) Zero product improvement time

c) Zero setup time

d) Zero purchasing time

63. Just in time arrangements with suppliers is associated with:

a) Zero customer feedback time

b) Zero product improvement time

c) Zero setup time

d) Zero purchasing time

64. The company should be able to manufacturer any of its products as soon as they are ordered is called:

a) Zero customer feedback time

b) Zero product improvement time

c) Zero setup time

d) Zero purchasing time

65. "The product should be free from any flaw" is called:

a) Zero customer feedback time

b) Zero product improvement time

c) Zero setup time

d) Zero Defects

66. All the activities involved in gathering market intelligence, disseminating it within the organization and acting on the information is called:

a) Market sensing process

b) New offering realization process

c) Customer acquisition process

d) Customer relationship management process

67. All activities involved in researching, developing and launching new high quality offerings quickly and within budget is called:

a) Market sensing process

b) New offering realization process

c) Customer acquisition process

d) Customer relationship management process

68. Defining target markets and prospecting for new customers is called:

a) Market sensing process

b) New offering realization process

c) Customer acquisition process

d) Customer relationship management process

69. Activities involved in building deeper understanding, relationships and offerings to customers is called:

a) Market sensing process

b) New offering realization process

c) Customer acquisition process

d) Customer relationship management process

70. Activities involved in receiving and approving orders, shipping the goods on time and collecting payment is called:

a) Market sensing process

b) Fulfillment management process

c) Customer acquisition process

d) Customer relationship management process

71. A superior value delivery network is also called as:

a) Supply chain

b) Value chain

c) Value delivery

d) Resource leveling

72. Cognitive space falls under ______ segment of Holistic Marketing Framework.

a) Customer Focus and Value Exploration

b) Core Competencies and Value Exploration

c) Collaborative Network and Value Exploration

d) None of these

73. Competency Space falls under ______ segment of Holistic Marketing Framework.

a) Customer Focus and Value Exploration
b) Core Competencies and Value Exploration
c) Collaborative Network and Value Exploration
d) None of these

74. Resource Space Competency Space falls under ______ segment of Holistic Marketing Framework.
a) Customer Focus and Value Exploration
b) Core Competencies and Value Exploration
c) Collaborative Network and Value Exploration
d) None of these

75. Business domain is associated with ___________ segment of Holistic Marketing Framework.
a) Customer Focus and Value Exploration
b) Core Competencies and Value Creation
c) Collaborative Network and Value Exploration
d) Collaborative Network and Creation

76. The Holistic Marketing Framework is designed to address __________ key management questions.
a) One
b) Two
c) Three
d) Four

77. "How can a company identify new value opportunities" is addressed by:
a) Value exploration
b) Value creation
c) Value delivery
d) Both a & b

78. "How can a company efficiently create more promising new value offerings" is tackled through:
a) Value exploration
b) Value creation

c) Value delivery
d) None of these
79. "How can a company use its capabilities and infrastructure to deliver the new value offerings more efficiently" can be figured out by:
a) Value exploration
b) Value delivery
c) Value creation
d) None of these
80. Internal resource management falls under the domain of:
a) Customer Focus and Value Delivery
b) Core Competencies and Value Delivery
c) Collaborative Network and Value Delivery
d) Customer Focus and Value Exploration
81. ______ reflects existing and latent needs and includes dimensions such as the need for participation, stability, freedom and change.
a) Cognitive space
b) Competency space
c) Resource space
d) Both a & b
82. __________ can be described in terms of breadth-broad versus focused scope of business, and depth-physical versus knowledge based capabilities.
a) Cognitive space
b) Competency space
c) Resource space
d) Both a & b
83. Which of the following involves horizontal partnerships?
a) Cognitive space
b) Competency space
c) Resource space
d) Both a & b
84. Business realignment which is necessary for maximizing core com-

petencies involves ________ steps.

a) One

b) Two

c) Three

d) Five

85. Defining/Redefining is the business concept is the ________ step under Business realignment.

a) First

b) Second

c) Third

d) Fourth

86. Shaping/Reshaping the business scope is the ________ step under Business realignment.

a) First

b) Second

c) Third

d) Fourth

87. Positioning/Repositioning the company's brand identity is the ________ step under Business realignment.

a) First

b) Third

c) Fifth

d) Seventh

88. ____________ allows the company to discover who its customers are and how they behave.

a) Internal resource management

b) Customer relationship management

c) Relationship marketing

d) Business partnership management

89. __________ is highly responsible for integrating major business processes under value delivery system.

a) Internal resource management

b) Business partnership management
c) Customer relationship management
d) Value exploration

90. ________ allows a company to handle its complex relationships with its trading partners to source, process and delivery products under value delivery system.
a) Internal resource management
b) Business partnership management
c) Customer relationship management
d) Value exploration

91. ________ is the central instrument for directing and coordinating the marketing effort.
a) Marketing strategy
b) Marketing myopia
c) Marketing plan
d) Contingency marketing plan

92. Marketing plan operates at ________ levels.
a) Two
b) Four
c) Six
d) Eight

93. This lays out the target markets and the value proposition that will be offered, based on an analysis of the best market opportunities.
a) Tactical marketing plan
b) Conventional marketing plan
c) Contingency marketing plan
d) Strategic marketing plan

94. It specifies the marketing tactics, including product features, promotion, merchandising, pricing, sales, channels and service.
a) Tactical marketing plan
b) Conventional marketing plan
c) Contingency marketing plan

d) Strategic marketing plan

95. All the corporate headquarters undertake _______ planning activities.

a) Two
b) Three
c) Four
d) Five

96. ________ is considered as an impossible dream.

a) Mission
b) Vision
c) Goals
d) Business definition

97. Under Strategic planning __________ is considered as the second step.

a) Corporate planning
b) Business planning
c) Division Planning
d) Product planning

98. Under Strategic planning __________ is considered as the first step.

a) Corporate planning
b) Business planning
c) Division Planning
d) Product planning

99. Under Strategic planning __________ is considered as the third step.

a) Corporate planning
b) Business planning
c) Division Planning
d) Product planning

100. Under Strategic planning __________ is considered as the fourth step.

a) Corporate planning
b) Business planning
c) Division Planning
d) Product planning

101. Good mission statements have ____________ major characteristics.
a) Two
b) Three
c) Four
d) Five

102. A strategic business unit has ____________ characteristics.
a) Two
b) Three
c) Four
d) Five

103. Ansoff proposed a useful framework for determining new intensive growth opportunities called:
a) Product- market expansion grid
b) Production-market expansion grid
c) Managerial grid
d) BCG Matrix

104. Market penetration strategy as per the Ansoff's Product-Market Expansion Grid comes under the preview of:
a) Current markets and current products
b) New markets and current products
c) Current markets and new products
d) New markets and new products

105. Market development strategy as per the Ansoff's Product- Market Expansion Grid comes under the preview of:
a) Current markets and current products
b) New markets and current products
c) Current markets and new products

d) New markets and new products

106. Product development strategy as per the Ansoff's Product-Market Expansion Grid comes under the preview of:

a) Current markets and current products

b) New markets and current products

c) Current markets and new products

d) New markets and new products

107. Diversification strategy as per the Ansoff's Product-Market Expansion Grid comes under the preview of:

a) Current markets and current products

b) New markets and current products

c) Current markets and new products

d) New markets and new products

108. To evaluate new prospects, Companies mostly use:

a) Market opportunity analysis

b) Management by objectives

c) Third party audits

d) Internal audits

109. In order to make improvements in products or services, firms ask consumers for their suggestion is called:

a) Problem detection method

b) Ideal method

c) Consumption chain method

d) None of these

110. In order to make improvements in products or services, firms ask consumers to imagine an ideal version of the product or service is called:

a) Problem detection method

b) Ideal method

c) Consumption chain method

d) All of these

111. In order to make improvements in products or services, firms ask

consumers to chart their steps in acquiring, using and disposing of a product is called:

a) Problem detection method

b) Ideal method

c) Consumption chain method

d) All of these

112. Opportunity Matrix is the combination of:

a) Seriousness and Probability of Occurrence

b) Attractiveness and Success Probability

c) Attractiveness and Seriousness

d) Probability of Occurrence and Success Probability

113. Threat Matrix is the combination of:

a) Seriousness and Probability of Occurrence

b) Attractiveness and Success Probability

c) Attractiveness and Seriousness

d) Probability of Occurrence and Success Probability

114. A firm needs a strategy, consisting of marketing strategy, technology strategy and ________________

a) Contingency strategy

b) Sourcing strategy

c) Conventional strategy

d) Both a) and b)

115. Michael Porter has proposed ____________ no. of generic strategies.

a) One

b) Two

c) Three

d) Four

116. In which type of generic strategy the firms need less skill in marketing.

a) Focus

b) Differentiation

c) Cost Leadership
d) Both b) and c)

117. In which of the generic strategy firm develops multiple variety of products or services.
a) Focus
b) Differentiation
c) Cost Leadership
d) Both b) and c)

118. In case of focus strategy, the firm concentrates on:
a) Narrow market
b) Medium size market
c) Large size market
d) None of these

119. According to Porter, firms pursuing the same strategy directed to the same target market constitute of
a) Strategic group
b) Joint venture
c) Merger
d) Counter trade

120.In which type of strategic alliance, one company licenses another company to produce its products or two companies jointly market their complimentary products.
a) Promotional alliance
b) Logistics alliance
c) Pricing collaboration
d) Product or service alliance

121. When one company agrees to carry promotion for another company's products or service is called:
a) Promotional alliance
b) Logistics alliance
c) Pricing collaboration
d) Product or service alliance

122. Offerings logistics support to another firm is known as:
a) Promotional alliance
b) Logistics alliance
c) Pricing collaboration
d) Product or service alliance

123. When organizations come forward in order to view ability to form and manage partnerships as core skills is called:
a) Core skill upgradation
b) Relationship management
c) Partner relationship management
d) Collaborative amalgamation

124. According to McKinsey & Co., strategy is one of the ____________ elements in successful business practice.
a) Three
b) Five
c) Seven
d) Nine

125. According to McKinsey & Co., strategy consists of seven elements and among them first three are considered as:
a) Hardware of success
b) Software of success
c) Both a & b
d) None of these

126. According to McKinsey & Co., strategy consists of seven elements and among them last four are considered as:
a) Hardware of success
b) Software of success
c) Both a & b
d) None of these

127. According to McKinsey & Co., strategy consists of seven elements and among them first is called as:
a) Strategy

b) Structure
c) Systems
d) Style
128. According to McKinsey & Co., strategy consists of seven elements and among them second is called as:
a) Strategy
b) Structure
c) Systems
d) Style
129. According to McKinsey & Co., strategy consists of seven elements and among them third is called as:
a) Strategy
b) Structure
c) Systems
d) Style
130. According to McKinsey & Co., strategy consists of seven elements and among them fourth is called as:
a) Strategy
b) Structure
c) Systems
d) Style
131.______________contains tactical guidelines for the marketing programs and financial allocations over the planning period.
a) Marketing plan
b) Strategy
c) Marketing strategy
d) Planning
132. ______________ includes a sales forecast, an expense forecast and a break even analysis.
a) Situational analysis
b) Financial projections
c) Marketing strategy

d) Market trends

133. A ________ is unpredictable, short lived, and without social, economic and political significance.

a) Fad

b) Trend

c) Megatrends

d) None of these

134. A ____________ is a direction or sequence of events that has some momentum and durability.

a) Fad

b) Trend

c) Megatrends

d) None of these

135. In order to spot cultural shifts, firms offer:

a) Cultural forecasts

b) Social-cultural forecasts

c) Demographic forecasts

d) All of these

136. The United States was originally called a

a) Melting pot

b) Melting bowl

c) Whistle blow

d) Grape vine

137. The United States is also called as ___________ society

a) Melting bowl

b) Whistle blow

c) Grape vine

d) Salad bowl

138. ________ is the type of economy in which a new rich class and a growing mkiddle class demand new types of goods.

a) Industrial economies

b) Industrializing economies

c) Both a and b

d) Raw material exporting economies

139. ______________ economies which are rich markets for all sorts of goods.

a) Subsistence economies

b) Industrializing economies

c) Industrial economies

d) Raw material exporting economies

140. In ______________ type of economies, there are few opportunities for marketers.

a) Subsistence economies

b) Industrializing economies

c) Industrial economies

d) Raw material exporting economies

141. ______________ is an organized movement of citizens and governments to strengthen the rights and powers of buyers in a relation to sellers.

a) Capitalist movement

b) Democratic movement

c) Consumerist movement

d) All of the above

142. ___________ firms gather consumer and trade information, which they sell for a fee.

a) Syndicated service research firms

b) Custom marketed research firms

c) Specialty line marketing research firms

d) Both a and b

143. ____________ firms are hired to carry out specific projects.

a) Syndicated service research firms

b) Custom marketed research firms

c) Specialty line marketing research firms

d) None of these

144. ______________ firms provide specialized research services.

a) Syndicated service research firms

b) Custom marketed research firms

c) Specialty line marketing research firms

d) None of these

145. ______________ is the first step in marketing research process.

a) Define the problem

b) Define the problem and research objectives

c) Develop the research plan

d) Both b and c

146. ______________ is the third step in marketing research process.

a) Develop the research plan

b) Organizing

c) Collect the information

d) Analyze the information

147. ______________ is the fifth step in marketing research process.

a) Analyze the information

b) Present the findings

c) Make the decision

d) None of the above

148. Under observational research approach, when hours of footage are edited to 30 minute footage is known as

a) Highlight reel

b) Highlight heel

c) Highlight capture

d) Behavioural data

149. A focus group is a gathering of __________ to ______________ people who are carefully selected based on certain considerations.

a) 5 to 8

b) 6 to 10

c) 7 to 10

d) 8 to 12

150. The purpose of experimental research is to capture.
a) The cause
b) The effect
c) The cause and effect relationship
d) None of the above
151. Qualitative research techniques are relatively ____________ measurement approaches.
a) Structured
b) Unstructured
c) Mixed
d) Both a and b
152. Observing people using products, shopping, travelling and using cell phones is called
a) Behaviour mapping
b) Consumer journey
c) Camera journals
d) Shadowing
153. Photographing people within a space such as hospital waiting room etc. is called
a) Behaviour mapping
b) Consumer journey
c) Camera journals
d) Shadowing
154. Keeping track of all the interactions, a consumer has with a product of service is called
a) Behaviour mapping
b) Consumer journey
c) Camera journals
d) Story telling
155. Asking consumers to keep visual diaries of their activities and impressions related to a product is called
a) Unfocus groups

b) Story telling

c) Extreme user interviews

d) Camera journals

156. Interviewing a diverse group of people in order to explore ideas is called

a) Unfocus groups

b) Story telling

c) Extreme user interviews

d) Camera journals

157. People can be asked "what words come to mind when they hear the brands name" is associated to

a) Brand personification

b) Visualization

c) Word associations

d) Laddering

158. People are presented an incomplete stimulus and are asked to complete it is an example of

a) Visualization

b) Projective techniques

c) Laddering

d) Brand personification

159. The people are asked to develop a collage to depict their perceptions is called

a) Visualization

b) Projective techniques

c) Laddering

d) Brand personification

160. People can be asked to describe "what kind of person they think of when a brand is mentioned to them" is known as

a) Visualization

b) Projective techniques

c) Laddering

d) Brand personification

161. A sampling plan calls for ____________ decisions.

a) Two

b) Three

c) Four

d) Five

162. The statement "Who is to be surveyed?" comes under:

a) Sampling Unit

b) Sample Size

c) Sampling Procedure

d) Both a & b

163. The statement "How many people should be surveyed?" comes under:

a) Sampling Unit

b) Sample Size

c) Sampling Procedure

d) None of the above

164. ____________ involves stopping people at shopping malls or street corners and requesting an interview.

a) Arranged interviews

b) Intercept interviews

c) Clickstream

d) Research interviews

165. Personnel interviewing is the most __________ method.

a) Versatile

b) Inflexible

c) Obstinate

d) Adamant

166. ____________ is a set of measures that helps firms to quantify, compare, and interpret their marketing performance.

a) Marketing Audit

b) Marketing management

c) Marketing metrics
d) Healthy skepticism

167. ______ records how well the company is doing year after year on customer based measures.

a) Customer performance scorecard
b) Customer performance evaluation
c) Customer audit
d) Consumer evaluation scorecard

168. A company uses ________ to track the level of satisfaction of various constituents who have a critical interest on companies performance, its employees etc.

a) Stakeholder scorecard
b) Stakeholder performance scorecard
c) Stakeholder performance evaluation
d) None of these

169. ________ consists of measuring and evaluating actual sales in relation to goals.

a) Sales variance analysis
b) Microsales analysis
c) Sales analysis
d) Sales productivity

170. _________ measures the relative contribution of different factors to a gap in sales performance.

a) Sales variance analysis
b) Microsales analysis
c) Sales analysis
d) Sales productivity

171. ________ looks at specific products, territories, and so forth that failed to produce expected sales.

a) Sales variance analysis
b) Microsales analysis
c) Sales analysis

d) Sales productivity

172. Market share can be measured in __________ ways.

a) Two

b) Three

c) Four

d) Five

173. ____________ is the company's sales expressed as a percentage of total marker sales.

a) Overall market share

b) Served market share

c) Relative market share

d) Served market

174. _________ is its sales expressed as a percentage of the total sales to its served market.

a) Overall market share

b) Served market share

c) Relative market share

d) Served market

175. _________ is the market where all the buyers are able and willing to buy their products.

a) Overall market share

b) Served market share

c) Relative market share

d) Served market

176. __________ can be expressed as market share in relation to its largest competitior.

a) Overall market share

b) Served market share

c) Relative market share

d) Served market

177. Overall market share is:

a) Customer penetration* Customer loyalty* Customer selectivity*

Price selectivity

b) Customer perception* Customer loyalty* Customer selectivity* Price selectivity

c) Customer penetration* Customer loyalty* Customer selectivity* Price compatibility

d) Customer penetration* Customer objectivity* Customer selectivity* Price selectivity

178. The control chart model under marketing management comprises of:

a) Sales ratio and Time period

b) Sales volume and Time period

c) Sales ration and Time schedule

d) Sales volume and Timing selectivity

179. ________ is the first step for analyzing marketing profitability analysis.

a) Defining goals and objectives

b) Identifying functional expenses

c) Assigning functional expenses to marketing entities

d) Preparing profit and loss statement for each marketing entity

180. ________ is the second step for analyzing marketing profitability analysis.

a) Defining goals and objectives

b) Identifying functional expenses

c) Assigning functional expenses to marketing entities

d) Preparing profit and loss statement for each marketing entity

181. ________ is the third step for analyzing marketing profitability analysis.

a) Preparing balance sheet

b) Identifying functional expenses

c) Assigning functional expenses to marketing entities

d) Preparing profit and loss statement for each marketing entity

182. _______ is the set of consumers who profess a sufficient level of

interest in a market offer.

a) Potential market
b) Available market
c) Target market
d) Penetrated market

183. ______ is the set of consumers who have interest , income and access to a particular offer.

a) Potential market
b) Available market
c) Target market
d) Penetrated market

184. ________ is the part of the qualified available market the company decides to pursue.

a) Potential market
b) Available market
c) Target market
d) Penetrated market

185. ______is the set of consumers who are buying the company's product.

a) Potential market
b) Available market
c) Target market
d) Penetrated market

186. ________pays to compare the current level of market demand to the potential demand level.

a) Share penetration index
b) Market penetration index
c) Product penetration percentage
d) Sales budget

187. The comparison of current market share to its potential market share is called:

a) Share penetration index

b) Market penetration index
c) Product penetration percentage
d) Sales budget

188. Companies interested in market potential have a special interest in ________.

a) Sales quota
b) Market penetration index
c) Product penetration percentage
d) Sales budget

189. ________ is a sales goal set for a product line or company division.

a) Sales forecast
b) Sales budget
c) Sales quota
d) Market share

190. ________ is the conservative estimate of the expected volume of sales and is used primarily for making current purchasing, production and cash flow decisions.

a) Sales forecast
b) Sales budget
c) Sales quota
d) Market share

191. __________method calls for identifying all the potential buyers in each market and estimating their potential purchases.

a) Market buildup
b) Market potential
c) Total market potential
d) Multiple factor index

192. NAICS stands for:

a) North American Industry Classification System
b) North Australian Industry Classification System
c) North American Industry Class System
d) North Australian Industry Class System

193. NAICS classifies all manufacturing into ______ major industry sectors.

a) Ten
b) Fifteen
c) Twenty
d) Twenty Five

194. Each sector classified by NAICS is further broken into ________ digit hierarchical structure.

a) Two
b) Four
c) Six
d) Eight

195. _________ procedure provides detailed estimates broken down by product, territoryand customer.

a) Market potential
b) Forecasting
c) Grassroots forecasting
d) Pooling individual estimates

196. _________consists of breaking down past time series into four components (trend, cycle, seasonal and erratic).

a) Times series analysis
b) Exponential smoothing
c) Statistical demand analysis
d) Econometric analysis

197. ____________consists of projecting the next periods sales by combining an average of past sales and the most recent sales, giving more weight to the latter.

a) Times series analysis
b) Exponential smoothing
c) Statistical demand analysis
d) Econometric analysis

198. _____________consists of measuring the impact level of each of a

set of casual factors (income, price etc).

a) Times series analysis
b) Exponential smoothing
c) Statistical demand analysis
d) Econometric analysis

199. ________consists of building sets of equations that describe a system and proceeding to fit the parameters statistically.

a) Times series analysis
b) Exponential smoothing
c) Statistical demand analysis
d) Econometric analysis

200. Which of the following is not a determinant of Customer delivered value?

a) Product value
b) Image value
c) Logistics value
d) Services value

201. Which of the following is a determinant of Customer delivered value?

a) Total customer cost
b) Monetary Cost
c) Personnel value
d) All of these

202. ______________ is the difference between the prospective customer's evaluation of all the benefits and all the costs of an offering and the perceived alternatives.

a) Customer perceived value
b) Total customer value
c) Total customer cost
d) None of these

203. ____________ is the perceived monetary value of the bundle of economic, functional and psychological benefits customer expect from a

given market offerings.

a) Customer perceived value
b) Total customer value
c) Total customer cost
d) Personnel value

204. ____________is the bundle of costs customer expect to incur in evaluating, obtaining, using and disposing of the given market offering, including monetary, time, energy and psychic costs.

a) Total customer cost
b) Monetary Cost
c) Time cost
d) Energy cost

205. "Delivering profitable value" is written by:

a) John Michael
b) Michael Lanning
c) Andy Reinhardt
d) Nicole Harris

206. ____________consists of the whole cluster of benefits the company promises to deliver.

a) Loyalty
b) Value delivery system
c) Value proposition
d) Profitable value

207. ____________ includes all the experiences which the customer will have on the way to obtaining and using the offerings.

a) Loyalty
b) Value delivery system
c) Value proposition
d) Profitable value

208. The book "Competing on Value" is written by

a) George and Sloan
b) Gardyn and Fetto

c) Lisa and Radice

d) Simon and Maklan

209. __________ can track the customer satisfaction directly.

a) Conformance quality

b) Performance quality

c) Mystery shoppers

d) Periodic surveys

210. ____________ describes the net present value of the stream of future profits expected over the customer's life time purchases.

a) Relationship equity

b) Value equity

c) Customer lifetime value

d) Value management

211. __________ is the customer's objective assessment of the utility of an offering based on perceptions of its benefits relative to its costs.

a) Brand equity

b) Relationship equity

c) Value equity

d) All of the above

212. _____________ is the customer's subjective and intangible assessment of brand, above and beyond its objectively perceived value.

a) Brand equity

b) Relationship equity

c) Value equity

d) All of the above

213. _______________ is the customer's tendency to stick with the brand, above and beyond objective and subjective assessments of its worth.

a) Brand equity

b) Relationship equity

c) Value equity

d) All of the above

214. __________ is the ability of a company to meet each customers requirements.

a) Customization

b) Mass customization

c) Customer equity

d) Value management

215. Once a customer always a customer is an example of

a) Simple retention market

b) Permanent capture markets

c) Customer migration markets

d) Reactive markets

216. Customers can permanently be lost after each period is an example of

a) Simple retention market

b) Permanent capture markets

c) Proactive markets

d) Basic markets

217. Customers can leave and come back is an example of

a) Simple retention market

b) Permanent capture markets

c) Customer migration markets

d) Basic markets

218. The sales person simply sells the products is an example of

a) Basic marketing

b) Reactive marketing

c) Proactive marketing

d) Partnership marketing

219. The sales person sells the product and encourages the customer to call if he/she has any comments or complaints is an example of

a) Basic marketing

b) Reactive marketing

c) Proactive marketing

d) Partnership marketing

220. The sales person calls the customer to check whether the product is meeting expectations is an example of

a) Proactive marketing

b) Partnership marketing

c) Accountable marketing

d) Reactive marketing

221. The sales person contacts the customer from time to time with the suggestions about improved products is an example of

a) Proactive marketing

b) Partnership marketing

c) Accountable marketing

d) Reactive marketing

222. The company works continuously with its large customers to help improve their performance

a) Proactive marketing

b) Partnership marketing

c) Accountable marketing

d) Reactive marketing

223. ______________ are designed to provide rewards to customers who buy frequently and in substantial amounts.

a) Frequency programs

b) Partnership memos

c) Business databases

d) Customer requirements

224. ______________ is an organized collection of comprehensive information about individual customers.

a) Customer database

b) Database marketing

c) Customer mailing list

d) Business database

225. ______________ is the process of building, maintaining and using

customer databases for the purpose of contacting, transacting and building customer relationships.
a) Customer database
b) Database marketing
c) Customer mailing list
d) Business database

226. ____________ is a simple set of names, addresses and other information about the customers.
a) Customer database
b) Database marketing
c) Customer mailing list
d) Business database

227. ____________ would contain customer's past purchases, past volumes, prices, profits etc.
a) Customer database
b) Database marketing
c) Customer mailing list
d) Business database

228. ________ is a fundamental determinant of a person's want and behavior.
a) Culture
b) Subculture
c) Social class
d) Family of procreation

229. __________ provides more specific identification and socialization of members.
a) Culture
b) Subculture
c) Social class
d) Family of procreation

230. _________revealed that different ethnic and demographic niches did not always respond favorably to mass market advertising.

a) Multicultural marketing
b) Subculture
c) Social class
d) Family of procreation

231. A person's ___________consists of all the groups that have a direct or indirect influence on his/her attitudes or behavior.
a) Aspirational groups
b) Primary groups
c) Reference groups
d) Secondary groups

232. Groups having a direct influence on a person are called:
a) Aspirational groups
b) Primary groups
c) Membership groups
d) Secondary groups

233. Individuals with whom a person interacts fairly, continuously and informally are called
a) Aspirational groups
b) Primary groups
c) Membership groups
d) Secondary groups

234. _____________are those whose values or behavior an individual rejects.
a) Aspirational groups
b) Dissociative groups
c) Membership groups
d) Secondary groups

235. _____________ are those groups which a person hopes to join.
a) Aspirational groups
b) Primary groups
c) Membership groups
d) Secondary groups

236. ____________ consists of parents and siblings.
a) Membership groups
b) Opinion leader
c) Family of orientation
d) Family of procreation
237. ______________ consists of one's spouse and children.
a) Membership groups
b) Opinion leader
c) Family of orientation
d) Family of procreation
238. Consumers who experience time famine are prone to
a) Time constant
b) Money constant
c) Multitasking
d) None of these
239. Lifestyles are shaped partly by whether consumers are
a) Money constrained or time constrained
b) Money constrained and time constrained
c) Multitasking
d) Ideal self
240. ___________ developed two factor theory.
a) Freud
b) Herzberg
c) Maslow
d) Ouchi
241. ___________ is the tendency to interpret information in a way that will fit our preconceptions.
a) Selective retention
b) Subliminal perception
c) Selective attention
d) Selective distortion
242. Because of ___________ we are likely to remember good points

about a product we like and forget good points about competing products.

a) Selective retention
b) Subliminal perception
c) Selective attention
d) Selective distortion

243. A ____________ is a strong internal stimulus impelling to action.

a) Learning
b) Subliminal perception
c) Cues
d) Drive

244. ____________ represents minor stimuli that determine when, where and how a person response.

a) Drive
b) Cues
c) Discrimination
d) Selective attention

245. ____________ means that the person has learned to recognize differences in sets of similar stimuli and can adjust responses accordingly.

a) Temporary repository
b) Permanent repository
c) Selective distortion
d) Discrimination

246. ________________ refers to how and where information gets into memory.

a) Memory processes
b) Memory encoding
c) Memory decoding
d) Memory endorser

247. ________________ is the third stage in five stage model of the consumer buying process.

a) Information search

b) Evaluation of alternatives
c) Purchased decisions
d) Post purchase behaviour

248. ______________ is the fifth stage in five stage model of the consumer buying process.
a) Information search
b) Evaluation of alternatives
c) Post purchase behaviour audit
d) Post purchase behaviour

249. The milder research state is called
a) Heightened attention
b) Selective attention
c) Aggressive attention
d) Both b and c

250. A __________ is a descriptive thought that a person holds about something.
a) Belief
b) Selective attention
c) Aggressive attention
d) Selective retention

251. ______________posits that consumers evaluate products and services by combining their brand beliefs (positives and negatives) according to importance.
a) Expectancy value model
b) Buying behavior model
c) Decision process model
d) All the above

252. With ______________ consumer sets a minimum acceptable cutoff level for each attribute and chooses the first alternative that meets the minimum standard for all attributes.
a) Lexicographic heuristic
b) Elimination by aspects heuristic

c) Conjunction heuristic
d) None of these
253. With _________consumers choose the best brand on the basis of its perceived most important attribute.
a) Lexicographic heuristic
b) Elimination by aspects heuristic
c) Conjunction heuristic
d) None of these
254. With _____________ the consumer compares brands on an attribute selected probabilistically.
a) Lexicographic heuristic
b) Elimination by aspects heuristic
c) Conjunction heuristic
d) None of these
255. In ___________ the product does not perform up to expectations.

a) Physical risk
b) Social risk
c) Functional risk
d) Time risk
256. In ___________ the product pose a threat to the physical well-being of consumers.
a) Physical risk
b) Social risk
c) Functional risk
d) Psychological risk
257. In _____________ the product is not worth the price paid.
a) Physical risk
b) Financial risk
c) Functional risk
d) Psychological risk
258. In ___________ the products results in embarrassment from oth-

ers.

a) Physical risk

b) Social risk

c) Functional risk

d) Psychological risk

259. In ____________ the product affects the mental well-being of the user.

a) Physical risk

b) Social risk

c) Functional risk

d) Psychological risk

260. In __________ the failure of the product results in an opportunity cost of finding another satisfactory product.

a) Physical risk

b) Social risk

c) Functional risk

d) Time risk

261. Elaboration likelihood model was proposed by:

a) Richard Petty and Cacioppo

b) Edward Russo and Schoemaker

c) Matt Krantz and Verne

d) Robert Yoegel and Frook

262. __________ are rules of thumb or mental shortcuts in the decision process.

a) Heuristics

b) Noncompensatory models

c) Cues

d) Drives

263. Consumers base their predictions on the quickness and ease with which a particular example of an outcome comes to mind.

a) Availability heuristic

b) Representativeness heuristic

c) Anchoring and adjustment heuristic

d) All the above

264. Consumers base their predictions on how representative or similar the outcome is to other examples.

a) Availability heuristic

b) Representativeness heuristic

c) Anchoring and adjustment heuristic

d) All the above

265. Consumers arrive at an initial judgment and then make adjustments of that first impression based on additional information.

a) Availability heuristic

b) Representativeness heuristic

c) Anchoring and adjustment heuristic

d) All the above

266. ____________ refers to the manner by which consumers code, categorize and evaluate financial outcomes of choices.

a) Mental Accounting

b) Management Accounting

c) Financial Risk

d) Social Risk

267. The principles of mental accounting are derived in part from ________________.

a) Behavioural Theory

b) Situational Theory

c) Prospect Theory

d) Psychological Theory

268. ___________ maintains that consumers frame decision alternatives in terms of gains and losses according to a value function.

a) Behavioural Theory

b) Situational Theory

c) Prospect Theory

d) Psychological Theory

269. Marketers think about how they themselves would act and learn about stages in buying process for their products is called:
a) Introspective method
b) Retrospective method
c) Consumption system
d) Customer scenario

270. In ____________ method marketers locate customers who plan to buy the product and ask them to think out load about going through the buying process.
a) Introspective method
b) Prospective method
c) Consumption system
d) Customer scenario

271. Marketers interview a small number of recent purchasers, asking them to recall the events leading to their purchase is called:
a) Introspective method
b) Retrospective method
c) Consumption system
d) Customer scenario

272. In ____________ consumers are asked to describe the ideal way to buy the product.
a) Prescriptive method
b) Retrospective method
c) Consumption system
d) Customer scenario

273. Trying to understand the customer's behavior in connection with a product has been called mapping the customer's ____________.
a) Consumption system
b) Customer activity cycle
c) Customer scenario
d) Mental accounting

274. Customers consumption system is also known as:

a) Customer activity cycle
b) Customer scenario
c) Both a & b
d) Retrospective method

275. NAPM stands for:
a) National Association of Project Management
b) National Association of Purchasing Managers
c) National Association of Planning Managers
d) None of these

276. ________- demand is not much affected by change in prices.
a) Derived demand
b) Fluctuating demand
c) Inelastic demand
d) Elastic demand

277. The purchasing department reorders on a routine basis is called:
a) Straight rebuy
b) Modified rebuy
c) Systems buying
d) Both a & b

278. In ____________ the buyer wants to modify product specifications, prices, delivery requirements or other terms.
a) Straight rebuy
b) Modified rebuy
c) Systems buying
d) Both a & b

279. ___________ type of customers consider price as everything.
a) Price oriented customers
b) Solution oriented customers
c) Gold standard customers
d) Straight value customers

280. Customers want low prices but will respond to arguments about lower total cost or more dependable supply or service:

a) Price oriented customers
b) Solution oriented customers
c) Gold standard customers
d) Straight value customers

281. __________ type of customers wants best performance in terms of product quality, assistance, reliable delivery and so on.
a) Price oriented
b) Solution oriented
c) Gold standard
d) Straight value

282. ________type of customers wants a fairly permanent sole-supplier relationship with your company.
a) Price oriented customers
b) Solution oriented customers
c) Gold standard customers
d) Straight value customers

283. In which of the following purchaser's focus is on short term and tactical approach.
a) Buying orientation
b) Procurement orientation
c) Supply chain management orientation
d) Bottleneck approach

284. In which of the following cases buyers simultaneously seek quality improvements and cost reduction.
a) Buying orientation
b) Procurement orientation
c) Supply chain management orientation
d) Bottleneck approach

285. In which of the following cases purchasing's role is further broadened to become a more strategic, value adding operation.
a) Buying orientation
b) Procurement orientation

c) Supply chain management orientation
d) Bottleneck approach

286. These products have low value and cost to the consumer and involve little risk.
a) Leverage products
b) Routine products
c) Strategic products
d) Bottleneck products

287. These products have high value and cost to the customer but involve little risk of supply.
a) Leverage products
b) Routine products
c) Strategic products
d) Bottleneck products

288. These products have high value and cost to the customer and also involve high risk.
a) Leverage products
b) Routine products
c) Strategic products
d) Bottleneck products

289. These products have low value and cost to the customer but they involve some risk.
a) Leverage products
b) Routine products
c) Strategic products
d) Bottleneck products

290. Which of the following identified 08 stages of business buying decision process?
a) Robinson and Associates
b) Robert and Associates
c) Nicole and Associates
d) Angwin and Associates

291. The eight stages of business buying decision process are also known as:

a) Buy Steps

b) Purchase Phases

c) Buy Phases

d) Buy Model

292. Which of the following is the second phase under Buygrid Framework?

a) Problem recognition

b) General need description

c) Supplier search

d) Proposal solicitation

293. Which of the following is the fourth phase under Buygrid Framework?

a) Product specification

b) General need description

c) Supplier search

d) Proposal solicitation

294. Which of the following is the sixth phase under Buygrid Framework?

a) Product specification

b) Order routine specification

c) Supplier selection

d) Performance review

295. Which of the following is the eighth phase under Buygrid Framework?

a) Product specification

b) Order routine specification

c) Supplier selection

d) Performance review

296. ____________ is an approach to cost reduction in which components are studied to determine if they can be redesigned or standardized

or made by cheap methods of production.

a) Buying alliances

b) Product value analysis

c) Product specification

d) Commoditization

297. In __________markets, participants offer to trade goods or services.

a) Catalog

b) Vertical

c) Barter

d) Pure play

298. RFP stands for:

a) Requests for Purchase

b) Requests for Procurements

c) Requests for Partnerships

d) Requests for Proposals

299. In ___________company engineers use laboratory tests to estimate the product's performance characteristics.

a) Field value-in-use assessment

b) Compositional approach

c) Internal engineering assessment

d) Conjoint analysis

300. In ________customers are interviewed about cost elements associated with using the new product offering compared to an incumbent product.

a) Field value-in-use assessment

b) Compositional approach

c) Internal engineering assessment

d) Conjoint analysis

301. In _______________customers are asked what value they would put on potential market offerings.

a) Field value-in-use assessment

b) Compositional approach
c) Internal engineering assessment
d) Focus group value assessment

302. In ____________ customers are asked to place a direct value on one or more changes in the market offering.
a) Direct survey questions
b) Benchmarks
c) Compositional approach
d) Focus group value assessment

303. In ____________customers are asked to rank their preference for alternative market offerings or concepts.
a) Direct survey questions
b) Benchmarks
c) Compositional approach
d) Conjoint analysis

304. In __________customers are asked to attach a monetary value to each of three alternative levels of a given attribute.
a) Direct survey questions
b) Benchmarks
c) Compositional approach
d) Conjoint analysis

305. In __________customers are asked to rate the importance of different attributes and the supplier firms performance on these attributes.

a) Importance ratings
b) Benchmarks
c) Compositional approach
d) Conjoint analysis

306. Blanket contracts are sometimes also called as:
a) Stockful purchase plans
b) Stockless purchase plans
c) Vendor managed inventory

d) Replenishment programs

307. The shifting of ordering responsibility to suppliers in systems is called:

a) Stockful purchase plans

b) Stockless purchase plans

c) Vendor managed inventory

d) Replenishment programs

308. __________represents the extent to which a company is seen as able to make and sell products or conduct services.

a) Corporate expertise

b) Corporate trustworthiness

c) Corporate likability

d) Contractual transaction

309. __________represents the extent to which a company is seen as motivated to be honest, dependable and sensitive to customer needs.

a) Corporate expertise

b) Corporate trustworthiness

c) Corporate likability

d) Contractual transaction

310. _______represents the extent to which a company is seen as likable, attractive, prestigious and dynamic.

a) Corporate expertise

b) Corporate trustworthiness

c) Corporate likability

d) Contractual transaction

311. __________is similar to basic buying and selling but more adaptation by the seller and less cooperation and information exchange.

a) Bare bones

b) Contractual transaction

c) Cooperative systems

d) Mutually adaption

312. __________generally has low levels of trust, cooperation and inter-

action.
a) Bare bones
b) Contractual transaction
c) Cooperative systems
d) Mutually adaption
313. Canon and Perreault found that buyer-supplier relationships differed according to ________ number of factors.
a) Three
b) Four
c) Five
d) Six
314. __________are those expenditures which are tailored to a particular company and value chain partner.
a) Specific investments
b) General investments
c) Investment patterns
d) Financing decisions
315. A flexible market offering consists of________parts.
a) One
b) Two
c) Four
d) Six
316. __________contains the product and service elements that all segment members' value.
a) Naked solution
b) Discretionary options
c) Preference segments
d) Homogeneous preferences
317. __________contains the product and service elements that some segment members' value.
a) Naked solution
b) Discretionary options

c) Preference segments
d) Homogeneous preferences
318. In which of the following cases consumers have same preferences:
a) Heterogeneous preferences
b) Homogeneous preferences
c) Diffused preferences
d) Clustered preferences
319. In which of the following cases consumers have scattered preferences:
a) Homogeneous preferences
b) Diffused preferences
c) Clustered preferences
d) Both b & c
320. In which of the following cases market might reveal distinct preference clusters.
a) Heterogeneous preferences
b) Homogeneous preferences
c) Diffused preferences
d) Clustered preferences
321. The cluster of small and middle sized firms in Germany is called:
a) Mittelstand
b) Mittstand
c) German Cloud
d) None of these
322. If a firm charges for stuff, it is in the ______________.
a) Commodity business
b) Goods business
c) Service business
d) Experience business
323. If a firm charges for tangible things, it is in the ______________
Commodity business
a) Goods business

b) Service business

c) Experience business

324. If a firm charges for activities it performs, it is in the ________________.

a) Commodity business

b) Goods business

c) Service business

d) Experience business

325. If a firm charges for the time spent with you, it is in the ________________.

a) Commodity business

b) Goods business

c) Service business

d) Experience business

326. Young, Single, married, older etc. is an example of

a) Family size

b) Density

c) Family life cycle

d) Social class

327. Lower lowers, upper lowers, working class, middle class etc. is an example of:

a) Social class

b) User status

c) Readiness stage

d) None of these

328. Unaware, aware, informed, interested, desirous, intending to buy etc. is an example of:

a) Loyalty status

b) Readiness stage

c) User status

d) Behavioural occasions

329. Couples or single headed households, most of them with kids, who

have decided to stay in urban centers rather than flee to the suburbs, are called:

a) Young Digerati

b) Beltway Boomers

c) The Cosmopolitans

d) Old Milltowns

330. ___________live in comfortable suburban subdivisions and are still pursuing kid centered lifestyles.

a) Young Digerati

b) Beltway Boomers

c) The Cosmopolitans

d) Old Milltowns

331. Which of the following households feature older homeowners, empty nesters and college graduates who enjoy leisure-intensive lifestyles.

a) Young Digerati

b) Beltway Boomers

c) The Cosmopolitans

d) Old Milltowns

332. These home centered residents make up one of the top segments for daytime television.

a) Young Digerati

b) Beltway Boomers

c) The Cosmopolitans

d) Old Milltowns

333. In ______________ buyers are divided into different groups on the basis of personality traits, lifestyle or values.

a) Psychological Segmentation

b) Behavioural Segmentation

c) Sequential Segmentation

d) Demographic Segmentation

334. The people whose purchases often reflect cultivated tastes for rel-

atively upscale, niche oriented products and services are called
a) Thinkers
b) Achievers
c) Strivers
d) Innovators
335. These people are mature, satisfied and are motivated by ideals and value order, knowledge and responsibility.
a) Innovators
b) Experiencers
c) Thinkers
d) Achievers
336. These people have successful goals and focus on career and family. They favor premium products that demonstrate success to their peers.
a) Achievers
b) Experiencers
c) Believers
d) Makers
337. These people are young, enthusiastic and impulsive who seek variety and excitement.
a) Achievers
b) Believers
c) Experiencers
d) Survivors
338. These are conservative, conventional and traditional type people with concrete beliefs.
a) Achievers
b) Believers
c) Experiencers
d) Survivors
339. These are trendy and fun loving people who are resource constraints.
a) Strivers

b) Makers

c) Believers

d) Survivors

340. These people are practical, down to earth and self-sufficient who like to work with their hands.

a) Believers

b) Achievers

c) Makers

d) Thinkers

341. These are elderly and passive people who are concerned about change. They are loyal to their favorite brands.

a) Believers

b) Achievers

c) Survivors

d) Thinkers

342. __________ segments prefer premium products and quality service.

a) True blues

b) Home bodies

c) Generation F

d) Road warriors

343. __________ segment of people accounts for fast fuel, fast service and fast food.

a) True blues

b) Home bodies

c) Generation F

d) Road warriors

344. ____________ segments prefer branded products and reliable service.

a) True blues

b) Price shoppers

c) Hardcore loyals

d) Split loyals

345. ____________ segments consider convenience at large.

a) Road warriors

b) Price shoppers

c) Home bodies

d) Shifting loyals

346. ____________ segments prefer low price.

a) Road warriors

b) Price shoppers

c) Home bodies

d) Shifting loyals

347. The consumers who buy only one brand all the time are called as:

a) True blues

b) Hardcore loyals

c) Sophisticates

d) Strategic value customers

348. The consumers who are loyal to more than one brand are called:

a) Shifting loyals

b) Switchers

c) Split loyals

d) Price shoppers

349. The consumers who show no loyalty to any brand are called as:

a) Shifting loyals

b) Split loyals

c) Switchers

d) None of these

350. The consumers who shift loyalty from one brand to another are called:

a) Shifting loyals

b) Split loyals

c) Switchers

d) None of these

351. Customers who have not yet purchased but want to buy from a vendor who understands their business, who explains things well and whom they can trust are called
a) Novices
b) Sophisticates
c) First time prospects
d) Price oriented customers
352. Customers who are starting their purchasing relationship want easy to read manuals, hotlines, a high level of training and knowledgeable sales representatives are called
a) Novices
b) Sophisticates
c) First time prospects
d) Strategic value customers
353. The established customers who want speed in maintenance and repair, product customization and high technical support are called as
a) Novices
b) Sophisticates
c) First time prospects
d) Strategic value customers
354. The customers who want value through lowest price are called
a) Sophisticates
b) Price oriented customers
c) Solution oriented customers
d) Strategic value customers
355. Customers who want value through more benefits and advice are called as
a) Sophisticates
b) Price oriented customers
c) Solution oriented customers
d) Strategic value customers
356. Customers who want value through supplier co–investing and

participating in the customer's business are called as
a) Experiencers
b) Price oriented customers
c) Solution oriented customers
d) Strategic value customers
357. Selling a product to price oriented customers is called
a) Enterprise selling
b) Consultative selling
c) Transactional selling
d) Segment attractiveness
358. Selling a product to solution oriented customers is called as
a) Enterprise selling
b) Consultative selling
c) Transactional selling
d) Segment attractiveness
359. Selling a product to strategic value customer is called as
a) Enterprise selling
b) Consultative selling
c) Transactional selling
d) Segment attractiveness
360. In ____________ the customers are grouped into segments based on similar needs and benefits sort by them
a) Segment identification
b) Segment attractiveness
c) Need based segmentation
d) Segment profitability
361. In ____________ it is determined which demographics, lifestyles and usage behaviour makes the segment distinct and identifiable.
a) Segment identification
b) Segment positioning
c) Marketing mix strategy
d) Segment Acid Test

362. ______________ uses predetermined segment attractiveness criteria to determine the overall attractiveness of each segment.

a) Segment identification

b) Segment positioning

c) Marketing mix strategy

d) Segment attractiveness

363. Which of the following determines the segment productivity?

a) Segment identification

b) Segment positioning

c) Marketing mix strategy

d) Segment profitability

364. ______________ creates a value proposition based on unique customer needs and characteristics.

a) Segment identification

b) Segment positioning

c) Marketing mix strategy

d) Segment profitability

365. ______________ is used to test the attractiveness of each segments positioning strategy.

a) Segment identification

b) Segment positioning

c) Marketing mix strategy

d) Segment Acid Test

366. ______________ expands segment position strategy to include all aspects if the marketing mix.

a) Segment identification

b) Segment positioning

c) Marketing mix strategy

d) Segment Acid Test

367. Which of the following is not an effective segmentation criteria.

a) Measurable

b) Substantial

c) Differentiable

d) Promotional

368. A ______________ is a set of segments sharing some exploitable similarity.

a) Segment identification

b) Super segment

c) Segregated segment

d) None of the above

369. When a firm makes a certain product that it sells to several different market segments, is called

a) Full market coverage

b) Differentiated marketing

c) Product specialization

d) Market specialization

370. In ____________ the firm concentrates on serving many needs of a particular customer group.

a) Full market coverage

b) Differentiated marketing

c) Product specialization

d) Market specialization

371. In ____________ the firm attempts to serve all customer groups with all the products they might need.

a) Selective specialization

b) Market specialization

c) Both a and b

d) Full market coverage

372. In ______________ the firm ignores segment differences and goes after whole market with one offer.

a) Undifferentiated marketing

b) Differentiated marketing

c) Societal marketing

d) Holistic marketing

373. In __________ the firm operates in several market segments and design different products for each segment.

a) Undifferentiated marketing

b) Differentiated marketing

c) Societal marketing

d) Holistic marketing

374. __________ cost accounts for changing a product to meet different market segment requirements and usually involves R & D and engineering.

a) Product modification

b) Manufacturing

c) Administrative

d) Inventory

375. If a product is sold in sufficiently large volume, __________ costs may be small per unit.

a) Product modification

b) Manufacturing

c) Administrative

d) Inventory

376. __________ cost is incurred while performing extra marketing research, forecasting, sales analysis, promotion, planning and channel management.

a) Product modification

b) Manufacturing

c) Administrative

d) Inventory

377. __________ is the added value endowed to products and services.

a) Brand equity

b) Customer based brand equity

c) Brand knowledge

d) Brand promise

378. __________ can be defined as the differential effect that brand

knowledge has on consumer response to the marketing of that brand.

a) Brand equity

b) Customer based brand equity

c) Brand knowledge

d) Brand promise

379. ______________ consists of all the thoughts, feelings, images, experiences and beliefs associated with the brand.

a) Brand equity

b) Customer based brand equity

c) Brand knowledge

d) Brand promise

380. ____________ is the marketer's reason of what the brand must be and do for consumers.

a) Brand promise

b) Brand strength

c) Brand identity

d) Brand stature

381. ____________ measures the degree to which a brand is seen as different from others.

a) Differentiation

b) Brand strength

c) Brand knowledge

d) Brand attributes

382. ______________ measures the breath of a brand's appeal.

a) Differentiation

b) Relevance

c) Esteem

d) Knowledge

383. ____________ measures how well the brand is regarded and respected.

a) Differentiation

b) Relevance

c) Esteem
d) Knowledge

384. ____________ measures how familiar and intimate consumers are with the brand.
a) Differentiation
b) Relevance
c) Esteem
d) Knowledge

385. Differentiation and relevance are combined to determine ____________
a) Brand strength
b) Brand performance
c) Brand stature
d) Brand performance

386. Esteem and knowledge are combined together to create ____________
a) Brand strength
b) Brand performance
c) Brand stature
d) Brand performance

387. ____________ is the unique set of brand associations that represents what the brand stands for and promises to customers.
a) Brand loyalty
b) Brand associations
c) Brand awareness
d) Brand identity

388. As per Aaker, brand identity consists of ________ dimensions.
a) 6
b) 12
c) 18
d) 24

389. As per Aaker, brand identity consists of ________ perspectives.

a) 4
b) 8
c) 12
d) 16

390. A world class car with employees who treat customers with respect and as friends represents their
a) Brand salience
b) Core identity
c) Brand resonance
d) Bonding

391. Which of the following questions represents “Presence” attributes of a brand?
a) Do I know about it?
b) Does it offer me something?
c) Does it offer something better than others?
d) Nothing else beats it?

392. Which of the following questions represents “Relevance” of a brand?
a) Do I know about it?
b) Does it offer me something?
c) Does it offer something better than others?
d) Nothing else beats it?

393. Which of the following questions represents “Performance” linked to a brand?
a) Do I know about it?
b) Does it offer me something?
c) Does it offer something better than others?
d) Can it deliver?

394. Which of the following questions represents “Advantage” linked to a brand?
a) Do I know about it?
b) Does it offer me something?

c) Does it offer something better than others?
d) Can it deliver?

395. Which of the following questions represents "Bonding" of a brand?

a) Do I know about it?
b) Does it offer me something?
c) Does it offer something better than others?
d) Nothing else beats it?

396. ____________ relates to how often and easily the brand is evoked under various purchase or consumption situations.

a) Brand performance
b) Brand judgments
c) Brand resonance
d) Brand salience

397. ____________ relates to how the product or service meets customer's functional needs.

a) Brand feelings
b) Brand judgments
c) Brand performance
d) Brand strength

398. ____________ deals with the extrinsic properties of product or service.

a) Brand feelings
b) Brand judgments
c) Brand performance
d) Brand imagery

399. ____________ focus on customer's own personnel opinions and evaluations.

a) Brand feelings
b) Brand judgments
c) Brand performance
d) Brand imagery

400. ____________ is/are customer's emotional responses and reactions with respect to the brand.
a) Brand feelings
b) Brand judgments
c) Brand performance
d) Brand imagery
401. There are __________ main sets of brand equity drivers.
a) One
b) Two
c) Three
d) Four
402. ______________ is/are those trademarkable devices that serve to identify and differentiate the brand.
a) Brand imagery
b) Brand resonance
c) Brand elements
d) Brand performance
403. How aesthetically appealing do consumers find the brand element represents:
a) Protectibility
b) Likeability
c) Memorability
d) Transferability
404. The question "What images come to mind?" represents
a) Association tests
b) Learning tests
c) Memory tests
d) Preference tests
405. The question "How easily is the name pronounced?" represents
a) Association tests
b) Learning tests
c) Memory tests

d) Preference tests

406. The question "How well is the name recognized?" represents

a) Association tests

b) Learning tests

c) Memory tests

d) Preference tests

407. The question "Which names are given preference?" represents

a) Association tests

b) Learning tests

c) Memory tests

d) Preference tests

408. __________ is about making sure that the brand and its marketing are as relevant as possible to as many customers as possible

a) Integrating marketing

b) Holistic marketing

c) Relationship marketing

d) Personalizing marketing

409. ___________ is about mixing and matching marketing activities to maximize their individual and collective effects.

a) Integrating marketing

b) Holistic marketing

c) Relationship marketing

d) Personalizing marketing

410. ___________ is consumer's ability to identify the brand under different conditions as reflected by their recall performance.

a) Brand image

b) Brand awareness

c) Internal branding

d) Brand bonding

411. _____________ is the perceptions and beliefs held by consumers as reflected in the associations held in consumer memory.

a) Brand image

b) Brand awareness
c) Internal branding
d) Brand bonding

412. __________ is the activities and processes that help to inform and inspire employees.
a) Internal branding
b) Brand bonding
c) Brand inventory
d) Brand audit

413. __________ occurs when customers experience the company as delivering on its brand promise.
a) Internal branding
b) Brand bonding
c) Brand inventory
d) Brand audit

414. __________ assesses potential sources of brand equity by identifying and tracking consumer brand knowledge structures.
a) Brand audit
b) Brand inventory
c) Direct approach
d) Indirect approach

415. __________ assesses the actual impact of brand knowledge on consumer response to different aspects of the marketing.
a) Brand audit
b) Brand inventory
c) Direct approach
d) Indirect approach

416. __________ is a consumer focused exercise that involves a series of procedures to assesses the health of brand or uncover its sources of brand equity and suggest ways to improve equity.
a) Brand audit
b) Brand inventory

c) Brand valuation

d) Brand reinforcement

417. ______________ is to provide a current, comprehensive profile of how all the products and services sold by a company are marketed and branded.

a) Brand audit

b) Brand inventory

c) Brand valuation

d) Brand reinforcement

418. ______________ is the research activity conducted to understand what consumers think and feel about the brand and its corresponding product category to identify sources of brand equity.

a) Brand tracking studies

b) Brand valuation

c) Brand exploratory

d) Brand revitalization

419. ______________ collects information from consumers on the routine basis over time.

a) Brand tracking

b) Brand revitalization

c) Brand knowledge

d) Brand extension

420. ______________ represents estimating the total financial value of the brand.

a) Brand valuation

b) Brand audit

c) Brand earnings

d) None of the above

421. ______________ requires innovation and relevance throughout the marketing program.

a) Brand reinforcement

b) Brand tracking

c) Brand leadership
d) Branding

422. When a firm uses an established brand to introduce a new product, it is called:
a) Brand extension
b) Sub brand
c) Parent brand
d) Category extension

423. When a new brand is combined with an existing brand, the brand extension can also be called as:
a) Family brand
b) Sub brand
c) Brand mix
d) Branded variants

424. An existing brand that gives birth to a brand extension is referred to as
a) Parent brand
b) Category extension
c) Brand mix
d) Brand variants

425. If the parent brand is already associated with multiple products through brand extensions, it may be called
a) Line extension
b) Category extension
c) Family brand
d) Brand mix

426. In ______________, the parent brand is used to brand a new product that targets a new market segment with in a product category currently served by the parent brand.
a) Line extension
b) Category extension
c) Family brand

d) Brand mix

427. In ________ the parent brand is used to enter a different product category from that currently served by the parent brand.

a) Line extension

b) Category extension

c) Family brand

d) Brand mix

428. ________ consists of all products (original as well as line and category extensions) sold under a particular brand.

a) Brand line

b) Brand mix

c) Brand width

d) Brand depth

429. A brand mix is also called as

a) Brand variants

b) Parent brand

c) Branding

d) Brand assortment

430. A ________ is the set of all brand lines, a particular seller makes available to buyer.

a) Brand variants

b) Parent brand

c) Brand mix

d) Brand assortment

431. ________are specific brand lines supplied to specific distribution channels.

a) Branded variants

b) Brands

c) Brand extensions

d) Brand categories

432. ________occurs when consumers no longer associate a brand with a specific product and start thinking less of the brand.

a) Brand assortment
b) Brand dilution
c) Brand crisis
d) Brand downfall

433. ____________is the set of all brands and brand lines a particular firm offers for sale to buyers in a particular category.
a) Brand portfolio
b) Brand renaissance
c) Brand revitalization
d) None of these

434. Fighter brands are also called as:
a) High end prestige brands
b) Cash cows
c) Flankers
d) Both b & c

435. High profitable brands are also called as:
a) Flankers
b) Cash cows
c) Flagships
d) High end prestige brands

436. ____________is the act of designing the companies offering and image to occupy a distinctive place in the mind of target market.
a) Positioning
b) Segmentation
c) Target market enrichment
d) Differentiation

437. The result of positioning is the successful creation of
a) Brand based value proposition
b) Customer based value proposition
c) Marketer based value proposition
d) Competition based value proposition

438. A starting point in defining a competitive frame of reference for a

brand positioning is to determine:
a) Category membership
b) Line membership
c) Value proposition
d) Points of Parity
439. __________ is/are attributes consumers strongly associate with a brand, evaluate positively and consider that they can't find the same with a competitive brand.
a) Points of parity
b) Points of difference
c) Leverage equity
d) Both a & b
440. Points of parity association comes in ________forms.
a) Two
b) Three
c) Four
d) Six
441. ____________ is/are the associations that are not necessarily unique to the brand but may in fact be shared with other brands.
a) Points of parity
b) Points of difference
c) Leverage equity
d) Both b & c
442. The two basic forms of points of parity are called:
a) Category and Competitive
b) Category and Differentiation
c) Focus and Differentiation
d) Category and Diversification
443. ____________represents necessary but not necessarily sufficient conditions for brand choice.
a) Category point of parity
b) Competitive point of parity

c) Point of difference

d) None of these

444. ___________ is/are associations designed to negate competitors points of difference.

a) Category point of parity

b) Competitive point of parity

c) Point of difference

d) None of these

445. There are __________ key consumer desirability criteria for points of difference.

a) Two

b) Three

c) Four

d) Five

446. There are __________ key deliverability criteria for points of difference.

a) Two

b) Three

c) Four

d) Five

447. Two important considerations that consumers find during analysis of points of difference are

a) Desirability and delivery

b) Desirability and measurability

c) Delivery and value proposition

d) Value creation and value delivery

448. ___________ is the way a company aims to identify or position itself or its product.

a) Differentiation

b) Image

c) Identity

d) Focus

449. __________ is the way public perceives the company or its products.

a) Differentiation

b) Image

c) Identity

d) Focus

450. A period of slow sales growth is witnessed in

a) Introduction stage

b) Growth stage

c) Maturity stage

d) Late maturity stage

451. The market in which buyers preferences scatter evenly is called:

a) Diffused Preference market

b) Single niche strategy

c) Multiple niche strategy

d) Mass market strategy

452. The strategy in which new product can be designed to meet the preferences of one of the corners of the market is called:

a) Diffused Preference market

b) Single niche strategy

c) Multiple niche strategy

d) Mass market strategy

453. The strategy in which two or more products can be simultaneously launched to capture two or more parts of the market is called:

a) Diffused Preference market

b) Single niche strategy

c) Multiple niche strategy

d) Mass market strategy

454. The strategy in which new product can be designed for the middle of the market is called:

a) Diffused Preference market

b) Single niche strategy

c) Multiple niche strategy
d) Mass market strategy
455. Market fragmentation is often followed by:
a) Market consolidation
b) Shadow pricing
c) Pure monopoly
d) Oligopoly
456. In ________only one firm provides a certain product or service in a certain country or area.
a) Pure Monopoly
b) Oligopoly
c) Pure Oligopoly
d) Differentiated Oligopoly
457. In __________ a small number of large firms produce products that range from high differentiated to standardized.
a) Pure Monopoly
b) Oligopoly
c) Pure Oligopoly
d) Differentiated Oligopoly
458. ___________consists of a few companies producing essentially the same commodity.
a) Pure Monopoly
b) Oligopoly
c) Pure Oligopoly
d) Differentiated Oligopoly
459. ____________consists of a few companies producing products partially differentiated along lines of quality, features, services etc.
a) Pure Monopoly
b) Oligopoly
c) Pure Oligopoly
d) Differentiated Oligopoly
460. In _______________many competitors are able to differentiate

their offers in whole or in part.
a) Monopoly
b) Pure competition
c) Monopolistic competition
d) Oligopoly
461. In ____________ many competitors offer the same product and service.
a) Monopoly
b) Pure competition
c) Monopolistic competition
d) Oligopoly
462. A group of firms following the same strategy in a given target market is called:
a) Strategic group
b) Strategic Mapping
c) Joint venture
d) Merger
463. A firm uses ____________ strategy for those new users who might use the product but do not use it.
a) Market penetration strategy
b) New market segment strategy
c) Geographical expansion strategy
d) Differentiation
464. A firm uses ____________ strategy for those new users who never use the product.
a) Market penetration strategy
b) New market segment strategy
c) Geographical expansion strategy
d) Differentiation
465. A firm uses ____________ strategy for those consumers who live elsewhere.
a) Market penetration strategy

b) New market segment strategy
c) Geographical expansion strategy
d) Differentiation

466. A/An ________marketer finds a stated need and fills it.
a) Responsive
b) Anticipative
c) Creative
d) Both a & b

467. A/An__________ marketer looks ahead into what needs customers may have in near future.
a) Responsive
b) Anticipative
c) Creative
d) Both a & b

468. A/An __________marketer discovers and produces solutions customers did not ask for but to which they enthusiastically respond.
a) Responsive
b) Anticipative
c) Creative
d) Both a & b

469. ___________involves shifting focus from the current product to the underlying generic need.
a) Market diversification
b) Market broadening
c) Planned contraction
d) Preannouncements

470. _________involves shifting into unrelated industries.
a) Market diversification
b) Market broadening
c) Planned contraction
d) Merger

471. In case of contraction defense _______________ is the best course

of action.
a) Market diversification
b) Market broadening
c) Planned contraction
d) Technological leapfrogging
472. Planned contraction is also known as:
a) Market diversification
b) Market broadening
c) Strategic withdrawal
d) Technological leapfrogging
473. In ____________ the attacker matches its opponents product, advertising, price, distribution etc.
a) Frontal attack
b) Flank attack
c) Encirclement attack
d) Bypass attack
474. In ____________ an enemy's weak spots are natural targets.
a) Frontal attack
b) Flank attack
c) Encirclement attack
d) Bypass attack
475. In ____________ the attempt is to capture a wide slice of the enemy's territory.
a) Frontal attack
b) Flank attack
c) Encirclement attack
d) Bypass attack
476. In ______________ the objective is to avoid the enemy and attacking easier markets to broaden the resource base.
a) Frontal attack
b) Flank attack
c) Encirclement attack

d) Bypass attack

477. ______________is a bypass strategy practiced in high-tech industries.

a) Frontal attack

b) Flank attack

c) Encirclement attack

d) Technological leapfrogging

478. ______________consists of waging small, intermittent attacks to harass and demoralize the opponent and eventually secure permanent footholds.

a) Frontal attack

b) Flank attack

c) Encirclement attack

d) Guerrilla warfare

479. A market challenger can launch a high quality product and charge a higher price than the leader is possible in case of:

a) Product innovation

b) Value priced goods

c) Prestige goods

d) Product proliferation

480. In ____________ the challenger can attack the leader by launching a large product variety.

a) Product innovation

b) Value priced goods

c) Prestige goods

d) Product proliferation

481. The ____________duplicates the leader's product and package and sells it on black market.

a) Counterfeiter

b) Cloner

c) Imitator

d) Adapter

482. The ___________emulates the leader's products, name and packaging with slight variations.
a) Counterfeiter
b) Cloner
c) Imitator
d) Adapter
483. The ___________copies something from the leader but maintains differentiation in terms of packaging, advertising, pricing or location.
a) Counterfeiter
b) Cloner
c) Imitator
d) Adapter
484. The ___________takes the leader's products and adapts or improves them.
a) Counterfeiter
b) Cloner
c) Imitator
d) Adapter
485. Positioning away from the dominant brand with a comparable or premium price and heavy advertising spending to establish the new brand as a credible alternative is called:
a) Challenger
b) Niche
c) Premium
d) Differentiation
486. Positioning close to the dominant brand with heavy advertising spending and comparable or premium price to challenge the dominant brand as the category standard is called:
a) Challenger
b) Niche
c) Premium

d) Differentiation

487. Positioning away from the dominant brand with a high price and a low advertising budget to exploit a profitable niche is called:

a) Challenger

b) Niche

c) Premium

d) Differentiation

488. Positioning near the dominant brand with little advertising spending but a premium price to move up market relative to the dominant brand is called:

a) Challenger

b) Niche

c) Premium

d) Differentiation

489. The marketer needs to address five product levels and those five constitute:

a) Core benefit

b) Consumption system

c) Customer value hierarchy

d) Potential product

490. The fundamental level from five product levels is:

a) Basic product

b) Expected product

c) Core benefit

d) Customer value

491. At the second product level the marketer has to turn the core benefit into:

a) Basic product

b) Expected product

c) Core benefit

d) Customer value

492. At third product level the marketer has to turn the basic product

into:
a) Basic product
b) Expected product
c) Core benefit
d) Customer value

493. At fourth product level the marketer has to turn the expected product into:
a) Basic product
b) Consumption system
c) Augmented product
d) Shopping goods

494. ___________is the way the user performs the tasks of getting and using products and related services.
a) Basic product
b) Consumption system
c) Augmented product
d) Shopping goods

495. _____________goods are purchased by consumers frequently, immediately and with minimum effort.
a) Convenience goods
b) Shopping goods
c) Specialty goods
d) Unsought goods

496. ___________are goods consumers purchase on regular basis.
a) Staples
b) Impulse goods
c) Emergency goods
d) Unsought goods

497. ___________goods are purchased without any planning or search effort.
a) Staples
b) Impulse goods

c) Emergency goods
d) Unsought goods
498. ___________goods are purchased when need is urgent.
a) Staples
b) Impulse goods
c) Emergency goods
d) Unsought goods
499. ____________are the goods purchased by following a selection process.
a) Shopping goods
b) Specialty goods
c) Unsought goods
d) Material and parts
500. ______________goods are similar in quality but different in price to justify shopping comparisons.
a) Homogeneous
b) Heterogeneous
c) Specialty
d) Unsought
501. ______________goods differ in product features and services that may be more important than price.
a) Homogeneous
b) Heterogeneous
c) Specialty
d) Unsought
502. ___________have unique characteristics for which a sufficient number of buyers are willing to make a special purchase effort.
a) Shopping goods
b) Specialty goods
c) Unsought goods
d) Material and parts
503. ____________are those the consumer does not know about or

normally does not think of buying.
a) Shopping goods
b) Specialty goods
c) Unsought goods
d) Material and parts related goods

504. __________ is the level at which the product's primary characteristics operate.
a) Performance quality
b) Conformance quality
c) Durability
d) Repairability

505. ______________is the degree to which all the produced units are identical and meet the promised specifications.
a) Performance quality
b) Conformance quality
c) Repairability
d) Reliability

506. __________is a measure of product's expected operating life under natural or stress conditions, is a valued attribute for certain products.
a) Durability
b) Style
c) Repairability
d) Reliability

507. _________ is a measure of the probability that a product will not fail within a specified time period.
a) Durability
b) Style
c) Repairability
d) Reliability

508. ___________is the measure of ease of fixing a product when it malfunctions.
a) Durability

b) Style
c) Repairability
d) Reliability

509. ___________refers to how easy it is for the customer to place an order with the company.
a) Delivery value
b) Zero response time
c) Ordering ease
d) Employee training

510. A group of products within the product family recognized as having a certain functional coherence is called:
a) Product class
b) Product mix
c) Product consistency
d) Product width

511. ___________refers to how many different product lines the company carries.
a) Product class
b) Product mix
c) Product consistency
d) Product width

512. ___________refers to total number of items in the mix.
a) Product class
b) Product mix
c) Product width
d) Product depth

513. ___________refers to how closely related the various product lines are in the end use, production requirements, distribution channels or some other way.
a) Product class
b) Product mix
c) Product consistency

d) Product depth

514. _________occurs when a company lengthens its product line beyond its current range.

a) Product innovation

b) Line stretching

c) Line filling

d) Product proliferation

515. A company positioned in the middle market may want to introduce a lower priced line is known as:

a) Down market stretch

b) Up market stretch

c) Two way stretch

d) Just noticeable difference

516. Companies enter into higher markets for more growth and higher margins accounts to:

a) Down market stretch

b) Up market stretch

c) Two way stretch

d) Just noticeable difference

517. Companies serving middle market might decide to stretch their line in all the directions is known as:

a) Down market stretch

b) Up market stretch

c) Two way stretch

d) Just noticeable difference

518. In ____________a product line can be lengthened by adding more items within the present range.

a) Down market stretch

b) Line stretching

c) Line filling

d) Just noticeable difference

519. _________occurs when a firm only offers its products as a bundle.

a) Bundling
b) Pure bundling
c) Mixed bundling
d) Differentiated bundling

520. In ____________the seller offers goods both individually and in bundles.
a) Bundling
b) Pure bundling
c) Mixed bundling
d) Differentiated bundling

521. ______________ involves creating brand equity for materials, components, or parts that are necessarily contained within other branded products.
a) Ingredient branding
b) Pure bundling
c) Mixed bundling
d) Differentiated bundling

522. All the activities of designing and producing the container for a product is called:
a) Packaging
b) Primary package
c) Secondary package
d) Shipping package

523. _______________are conducted to ensure that the package stands up under normal conditions.
a) Engineering tests
b) R&D tests
c) Visual tests
d) Dealer tests

524. ______________________are conducted to ensure that the script is legible and the colours harmonious.
a) Engineering tests

b) R&D tests
c) Visual tests
d) Dealer tests

525. ___________tests are conducted to ensure that distributors find the package attractive and easy to handle.
a) Engineering tests
b) R&D tests
c) Consumer tests
d) Dealer tests

526. _________tests are conducted to ensure that consumers provide favorable response.
a) Engineering tests
b) R&D tests
c) Consumer tests
d) Dealer tests

527. ___________is responsible for making the consumers describe the freshness of products.
a) Open dating
b) Unit pricing
c) Grade labeling
d) Percentage labeling

528. _________represents describing product cost in standard measurement units.
a) Open dating
b) Unit pricing
c) Grade labeling
d) Percentage labeling

529. _________is to rate the quality level.
a) Open dating
b) Unit pricing
c) Grade labeling
d) Percentage labeling

530. ____________is to show the percentage of each important ingredient.
a) Open dating
b) Unit pricing
c) Grade labeling
d) Percentage labeling
531. __________ is any act or performance that one party can offer to another that is essentially intangible and does not result in the ownership of anything.
a) Service
b) Experience
c) Creativity
d) Legal tender
532. Cars and computers are an example of:
a) Pure tangible goods
b) Tangible goods with accompanying services
c) Hybrid
d) Major service with accompanying minor goods and services
533. People patronize for both food and service is an example of:
a) Pure tangible goods
b) Tangible goods with accompanying services
c) Hybrid
d) Major service with accompanying minor goods and services
534. Airline passengers come in which of the following category;
a) Pure tangible goods
b) Tangible goods with accompanying services
c) Hybrid
d) Major service with accompanying minor goods and services
535. Soap, toothpaste, salt comes in which of the following category:
a) Pure tangible goods
b) Tangible goods with accompanying services
c) Hybrid

d) Major service with accompanying minor goods and services

536. ____________are the characteristics a buyer can evaluate before purchase.

a) Search qualities

b) Experience qualities

c) Credence qualities

d) None of these

537. ____________are the characteristics a buyer can evaluate after purchase.

a) Search qualities

b) Experience qualities

c) Credence qualities

d) None of these

538. ____________are the characteristics a buyer normally finds hard to evaluate.

a) Search qualities

b) Experience qualities

c) Credence qualities

d) None of these

539. ____________proposed the concept of customer experience engineering.

a) George and James

b) Carbone and Haeckel

c) Richard and Ravinson

d) Michael and Ansoff

540. "Services cannot be stored" represents their:

a) Intangibility

b) Inseparability

c) Variability

d) Perishability

541. ____________describes the normal work of preparing, pricing, distributing and promoting the service to customers.

a) Internal marketing
b) External marketing
c) Interactive marketing
d) Both a & b

542. __________describes training and motivating employees to serve customers well.
a) Internal marketing
b) External marketing
c) Interactive marketing
d) Both a & b

543. __________describes the employee's skill in serving the client.
a) Internal marketing
b) External marketing
c) Interactive marketing
d) Either a & b

544. The ability to perform the promised service dependably and accurately is called:
a) Reliability
b) Responsiveness
c) Assurance
d) Empathy

545. The willingness to help customers and to provide prompt service is called:
a) Reliability
b) Responsiveness
c) Assurance
d) Empathy

546. The knowledge of courtesy of employees and their ability to convey trust and confidence is called:
a) Reliability
b) Responsiveness
c) Assurance

d) Empathy

547. The provision of caring, individualized attention to customers is called:

a) Reliability

b) Responsiveness

c) Assurance

d) Empathy

548. The suppliers who are better at handling emergencies, product recalls, and answering inquiries represents their:

a) Innovativeness

b) Reliability

c) Resilience

d) Assurance

549. Setting up of low price for consumers accounts to:

a) Market skimming pricing

b) Market penetration pricing

c) Mark up pricing

d) Psychological pricing

550. Setting up of high price for consumers accounts to:

a) Market skimming pricing

b) Market penetration pricing

c) Mark up pricing

d) Psychological pricing

551. In service quality model, difference between expected service and management perception of consumer expectations is:

a) Gap 1

b) Gap 2

c) Gap 4

d) Gap 5

552. In service quality model, difference between service delivery and external communications to consumers is:

a) Gap 1

b) Gap 2

c) Gap 3

d) Gap 4

553. In service quality model, difference between service delivery and translation of perceptions into service quality specifications is:

a) Gap 1

b) Gap 2

c) Gap 3

d) Gap 4

554. In service quality model, difference between translation of perceptions into service quality specifications and management perception of consumer expectations is:

a) Gap 1

b) Gap 2

c) Gap 3

d) Gap 4

555. In service quality model, difference between expected service and perceived service is:

a) Gap 1

b) Gap 3

c) Gap 4

d) Gap 5

556. Fixed costs are also known as:

a) Sunk costs

b) Contingent costs

c) Overhead costs

d) Both b & c

557. Variable costs vary directly with:

a) Level of production

b) Revenue

c) Both a & b

d) None of these

558. In ___________the firm determines the price that would yield its target rate of return on investment.
a) Target return pricing
b) Value pricing
c) Penetration pricing
d) Competitor pricing
559. Marketers win loyal customers by charging a fairly low price for high quality offering:
a) Skimming pricing
b) Value pricing
c) Penetration pricing
d) Psychological pricing
560. The firm bases its price largely on competitors in:
a) Going rate pricing
b) Value pricing
c) Penetration pricing
d) Psychological pricing
561. Ascending bids are also called as:
a) English auctions
b) Dutch auctions
c) Sealed bid auctions
d) None of these
562. Descending bids are also called as:
a) English auctions
b) Dutch auctions
c) Sealed bid auctions
d) None of these
563. In ___________auctions would be suppliers can submit only one bid and cannot know the other bid.
a) English auctions
b) Dutch auctions
c) Sealed bid auctions

d) Both b & c

564. The direct exchange of goods with no money and no third party involves is called:

a) Compensation deal

b) Barter

c) Buyback arrangement

d) Offset

565. The seller receives some percentage of payment in cash and the rest in form of products is called:

a) Compensation deal

b) Barter

c) Buyback arrangement

d) Offset

566. The seller sells a plant, equipment or technology to another country and agrees to accept as partial payment products manufactured with the supplied equipment is called:

a) Compensation deal

b) Barter

c) Buyback arrangement

d) Offset

567. The seller receives full payment in cash but agrees to spend a substantial amount of the money in that country within a stated time period is called:

a) Compensation deal

b) Barter

c) Buyback arrangement

d) Offset

568. A price reduction to buyers who pay bills promptly is called:

a) Cash discount

b) Quantity discount

c) Functional discount

d) Seasonal discount

569. A price reduction to those who buy large volumes is called:
a) Cash discount
b) Quantity discount
c) Functional discount
d) Seasonal discount
570. Discount offered to channel members is called:
a) Cash discount
b) Quantity discount
c) Functional discount
d) Seasonal discount
571. An extra payment designed to gain reseller participation in special programs is called:
a) Cash discount
b) Allowance
c) Functional discount
d) Seasonal discount
572. Supermarkets and departmental stores often drop the price on well-known brands to stimulate additional store traffic is called:
a) Loss leader pricing
b) Special event pricing
c) Cash rebates
d) Psychological discounting
573. Sellers will establish special prices in certain seasons to draw in more customers is associated with:
a) Loss leader pricing
b) Special event pricing
c) Skimming pricing
d) Psychological discounting
574. __________involves setting up an artificially high price and then offering the product at substantial savings.
a) Customer segment pricing
b) Special event pricing

c) Cash rebates

d) Psychological discounting

575. __________occurs when a firm sells a product or service at two or more prices that do not reflect a proportional difference in costs.

a) Price discrimination

b) Customer segment pricing

c) Product form pricing

d) Shallow pockets trap

576. Different customer groups are charged different prices for the same product or service is called:

a) Price discrimination

b) Customer segment pricing

c) Product form pricing

d) Shallow pockets trap

577. Different versions of the product are priced differently but not proportionately to their respective costs is called:

a) Price discrimination

b) Customer segment pricing

c) Product form pricing

d) Shallow pockets trap

578. Some companies' price the same product at two different levels based on image differences is called:

a) Image pricing

b) Channel pricing

c) Location pricing

d) Time pricing

579. Coca Cola carries a different price depending on whether it is purchased in a fine restaurant, fast food restaurant or vending machine is called:

a) Image pricing

b) Channel pricing

c) Location pricing

d) Time pricing

580. Prices are varied by season, day or hour is an example of:

a) Image pricing

b) Channel pricing

c) Location pricing

d) Time pricing

581. Same product is charged differently at different locations even though the cost of offering is same is called:

a) Image pricing

b) Channel pricing

c) Location pricing

d) Time pricing

582. "Consumers will assume that the quality is low" accounts to:

a) Fragile market share trap

b) Shallow pockets trap

c) Low quality trap

d) Escalator clauses

583. "A low price buys market share not market loyalty" accounts to

a) Fragile market share trap

b) Shallow pockets trap

c) Low quality trap

d) Escalator clauses

584. The higher priced competitors may cut their prices and may have longer staying power because of deeper cash reserves is called:

a) Fragile market share trap

b) Shallow pockets trap

c) Low quality trap

d) Escalator clauses

585. The company does not set a final price until the product is finished or delivered is called:

a) Escalator clauses

b) Unbundling

c) Reduction of discounts
d) Delayed quotation pricing

586. The company requires the customer to pay today's price due to any circumstances before delivery is called:
a) Escalator clauses
b) Unbundling
c) Reduction of discounts
d) Delayed quotation pricing

587. The company maintains its price but removes or prices separately one or more elements that were part of the former offer such as free delivery or installation is called:
a) Escalator clauses
b) Unbundling
c) Reduction of discounts
d) Delayed quotation pricing

588. The company instructs its sales force not to offer its normal cash and quantity discounts is called:
a) Escalator clauses
b) Unbundling
c) Reduction of discounts
d) Delayed quotation pricing

589. ______________involves the manufacturer using its sales force and trade promotion money to induce intermediaries to carry, promote and sell the product to end users.
a) Pull strategy
b) Push strategy
c) Channel integration
d) Spatial convenience

590. ____________involves the manufacturer using advertising and promotion to persuade consumers to ask intermediaries for the product, thus inducing the intermediaries to order it.
a) Pull strategy

b) Push strategy
c) Channel integration
d) Spatial convenience

591. __________purchase from the same places in the same manner over time.
a) High value deal seekers
b) High involvement shoppers
c) Variety loving shoppers
d) Habitual shoppers

592. __________know their needs and "channel surf" a great deal before buying at the lowest possible price.
a) High value deal seekers
b) High involvement shoppers
c) Variety loving shoppers
d) Habitual shoppers

593. ____________gather information in many channels, take advantage of high-touch services and then buy in their favorite channel regardless of price.
a) High value deal seekers
b) High involvement shoppers
c) Variety loving shoppers
d) Habitual shoppers

594. ____________gather information in all channels, make their purchase in a low cost channel, but take advantage of customer support from a high-touch channel.
a) High value deal seekers
b) High involvement shoppers
c) Variety loving shoppers
d) Habitual shoppers

595. A direct marketing channel is also called as:
a) Zero level channel
b) Two tier channel

c) Three tier channel

d) Both a & b

596. A three tier level channel consists of ____________intermediaries.

a) Three

b) Four

c) Three + Two

d) None of these

597. The degree to which marketing channel makes it easy for customers to purchase the product is called:

a) Service backup

b) Product application

c) Spatial convenience

d) Intensive distribution

598. __________means severely limiting the number of intermediaries.

a) Intensive distribution

b) Exclusive distribution

c) Selective distribution

d) Economic criteria

599. __________involves the use of more than a few but less than all of the intermediaries who are willing to carry a particular product.

a) Intensive distribution

b) Exclusive distribution

c) Selective distribution

d) Economic criteria

600. __________consists of the manufacturer placing the goods or services in as many outlets as possible.

a) Intensive distribution

b) Exclusive distribution

c) Selective distribution

d) Economic criteria

601. ___________is the ability to alter channel member's behavior so that they take actions they would not have taken otherwise.

a) Channel Power

b) Economic Criteria

c) Legitimate Power

d) Referent Power

602. A manufacturer threatens to withdraw a resource or terminate a relationship if intermediaries fail to cooperate is an example of:

a) Legitimate power

b) Referent power

c) Coercive power

d) Reward power

603. The manufacturer offers intermediaries an extra benefit for performing specific acts or functions in

a) Legitimate power

b) Referent power

c) Coercive power

d) Reward power

604. The manufacturer requests a behavior that is warranted under the contract account to:

a) Legitimate power

b) Referent power

c) Coercive power

d) Reward power

605. The manufacturer has special knowledge that intermediaries value under:

a) Legitimate power

b) Referent power

c) Expert power

d) Reward power

606. The manufacturer is so highly respected that intermediaries are proud to be associated with it under:

a) Legitimate power
b) Referent power
c) Coercive power
d) Reward power

607. __________combines successive stages of production and distribution under single ownership.
a) Vertical marketing system
b) Administered vertical marketing system
c) Corporate vertical marketing system
d) Contractual vertical marketing system

608. ___________comprises the producer, wholesaler and retailer acting as a unified system.
a) Vertical marketing system
b) Administered vertical marketing system
c) Corporate vertical marketing system
d) Contractual vertical marketing system

609. ___________coordinates successive stages of production and distribution through size and power of one of the members.
a) Vertical marketing system
b) Administered vertical marketing system
c) Corporate vertical marketing system
d) Contractual vertical marketing system

610. The manufacturer establishes a department within the company called as:
a) Vertical marketing system
b) Distributor-relations planning
c) Corporate vertical marketing system
d) Contractual vertical marketing system

611. _________ consists of independent firms at different levels of production and distribution integrating their programs on a contractual basis to obtain more economies or sales impact than they can achieve alone.

a) Vertical marketing system
b) Administered vertical marketing system
c) Corporate vertical marketing system
d) Contractual vertical marketing system

612. ____________ is defined as building a plant, professionally managed, vertical marketing system that meets the need of both manufacturer and distributer is called
a) Vertical marketing system
b) Administered vertical marketing system
c) Corporate vertical marketing system
d) Distribution programming

613. The marketing system in which two or more unrelated companies put together resources or programs to exploit an emerging marketing opportunity.
a) Vertical marketing system
b) Horizontal marketing system
c) Corporate vertical marketing system
d) Distribution programming

614. __________ is generated when one channel member actions prevent the other channel from achieving its goal.
a) Channel conflict
b) Distribution programming
c) Diplomacy
d) Arbitration

615. ____________ means conflict between different levels within the same channel.
a) Vertical channel conflict
b) Horizontal channel conflict
c) Multichannel conflict
d) Both a and b

616. ____________ involves conflict between members at the same level within the channel.

a) Vertical channel conflict
b) Horizontal channel conflict
c) Multichannel conflict
d) Both a and b

617. __________ exists when the manufacturer has established to or more channels that sell to the same market.
a) Vertical channel conflict
b) Horizontal channel conflict
c) Multichannel conflict
d) None of these

618. __________ is an effort by one organization to win the support of the leaders of another organization.
a) Diplomacy
b) Mediation
c) Arbitration
d) Co-optation

619. ____________ takes place when each side sends a person or group to meet with its counterpart to resolve the conflict.
a) Diplomacy
b) Mediation
c) Arbitration
d) Co-optation

620. ___________ means resorting to a neutral third party who is skilled in conciliating the two party's interests.
a) Diplomacy
b) Mediation
c) Arbitration
d) Co-optation

621. ____________ occurs when the two parties agree to present their arguments to one or more arbitrators and accept the arbitration decision.
a) Diplomacy

b) Mediation
c) Arbitration
d) Co-optation

622. ____________ describes the use of electronic means to conduct a company's business.
a) E-commerce
b) E-business
c) E-marketing
d) E-purchasing

623. ____________ means that the company or site offers to transact or facilitate the selling of product and services online.
a) E-commerce
b) E-business
c) E-marketing
d) E-purchasing

624. ____________means companies decide to purchase goods, services and information from various online suppliers.
a) E-commerce
b) E-business
c) E-marketing
d) E-purchasing

625. ____________describes company efforts to inform buyers, communicate, promote and sell its products and services over the internet.
a) E-commerce
b) E-business
c) E-marketing
d) E-purchasing

626. ____________companies are those that have launched a website without any previous existence as a firm.
a) Pure click
b) Brick and Click
c) Both a & b

d) None of these

627. Existing companies that have added an online site for information and e commerce are called:

a) Pure click

b) Brick and Click

c) Both a & b

d) None of these

628. ___________ is/are third parties that create markets linking buyers and sellers.

a) Infomediaries

b) Market makers

c) Supplier website

d) Customer communities

629. ___________ is/are websites where buyers can swap stories about suppliers products and services.

a) Infomediaries

b) Market makers

c) Supplier website

d) Customer communities

630. ___________ includes all the activities involved in selling goods and services directly to final consumers for personal, non-business use.

a) Retailing

b) Wholesaling

c) Voluntary chain

d) Sunglass hut

631. ___________ explains one reason that new store types emerge.

a) Wheel of retailing hypothesis

b) Bloomingdale

c) Tiffany

d) Corporate retailing

632. ___________ have narrow product line.

a) Specialty store
b) Convenience store
c) Department store
d) Discount store

633. __________ have several product lines.
a) Specialty store
b) Convenience store
c) Departmental store
d) None of these

634. ___________ are the small stores in residential area.
a) Specialty store
b) Convenience store
c) Department store
d) Discount store

635. ___________ stores feature a broad product assortment and high value added.
a) Bloomingdale
b) Catalogue showroom
c) Sunglass hut
d) Tiffany

636. Stores that feature a narrow product assortment and high value added.
a) Bloomingdale
b) Catalogue showroom
c) Sunglass hut
d) Tiffany

637. __________ stores feature a narrow line and low value added.
a) Bloomingdale
b) Catalogue showroom
c) Sunglass hut
d) Tiffany

638. ___________ stores features a broad line and low value added.

a) Bloomingdale
b) Catalogue showroom
c) Sunglass hut
d) Wal-Mart

639. Direct selling is also called as
a) Direct marketing
b) Telemarketing
c) Automatic vending
d) Multilevel selling

640. Direct selling is also called as
a) Direct marketing
b) Telemarketing
c) Automatic vending
d) Network marketing

641. __________ is used for a variety of merchandise.
a) Direct marketing
b) Telemarketing
c) Automatic vending
d) Network marketing

642. __________ is used to measure a product's measuring costs from the time it reaches the warehouse until a customer buys it in the retail store.
a) Direct product profitability
b) Direct market profitability
c) Indirect product profitability
d) Indirect market profitability

643. Strip malls are also called as
a) General business districts
b) Community shopping centers
c) Departmental stores
d) Shopping strips

644. Many supermarkets charge a ____________ for accepting a new

brand to cover the cost of listing and stocking.
a) Awareness cost
b) Awareness fee
c) Slotting fee
d) Both a and b
645. _____________ are independently owned businesses that take title to the merchandise they handle.
a) Merchant wholesalers
b) Full service wholesalers
c) Brokers
d) Specialized wholesalers
646. _________ involves the planning the infrastructure to meet demand and then implementing and controlling the physical flow of material from point of origin to points of use.
a) Supply chain management
b) Market logistics
c) Enterprise resource planning
d) Warehouse
647. In __________ wholesalers recognize that their role is not simply to represent the supplier's interests or customer's but to support both.
a) Supply chain management
b) Market logistics
c) Enterprise resource planning
d) Marketing support philosophy
648. ___________ consists of putting the goods in trailers that are easy to transfer between two transportation modes.
a) Piggyback
b) Trainship
c) Fishyback
d) Containerization
649. ___________ is any paid form of non-personnel presentation and promotion of goods and services by an identified sponsor.

a) Advertising
b) Sales promotion
c) Public relation
d) Publicity

650. __________ is a variety of short-term incentives to encourage trial or purchase of products and services.
a) Advertising
b) Sales promotion
c) Public relation
d) Publicity

651. __________describes the use of rail and trucks in transportation.
a) Piggyback
b) Trainship
c) Airtruck
d) Contract carrier

652. ____________are company sponsored activities and programs designed to create daily or special brand related interactions.
a) Advertising
b) Personal selling
c) Direct marketing
d) Events and experiences

653. ____________is a variety of programs designed to promote or protect a company's image or its individual products.
a) Advertising
b) Personal selling
c) Direct marketing
d) Public relation and publicity

654. Face to face interaction with one or more prospective purchasers for the purpose of making presentations, answering questions and procuring orders is called:
a) Advertising
b) Personal selling

c) Direct marketing

d) Public relation and publicity

655. ____________are how marketers translate their messages into a specific communication.

a) Creative strategies

b) Informational appeals

c) Transformational appeals

d) Principle of congruity

656. ____________elaborates on product or service attributes or benefits.

a) Creative strategies

b) Informational appeals

c) Transformational appeals

d) Principle of congruity

657. __________elaborates on a non-product related benefit or image.

a) Creative strategies

b) Informational appeals

c) Transformational appeals

d) Principle of congruity

658. __________implies that communicators can use their good image to reduce some negative feelings toward a brand but in the process might lose some esteem with the audience.

a) Creative strategies

b) Informational appeals

c) Transformational appeals

d) Principle of congruity

659. __________represents that advertising permits the seller to repeat a message many times.

a) Pervasiveness

b) Amplified expressiveness

c) Impersonality

d) High credibility

660. ________represents that advertising provides opportunities for dramatizing the company and its products through the artful use of print, sound and color.
a) Pervasiveness
b) Amplified expressiveness
c) Impersonality
d) High credibility
661. The audience does not feel obligated to pay attention or respond to advertising accounts to:
a) Pervasiveness
b) Amplified expressiveness
c) Impersonality
d) High credibility
662. When sales representatives persuade dealers to take more stock and devout more shelf space to the company's brand is called
a) Increased stock position
b) Enthusiasm building
c) Missionary selling
d) Key account management
663. In ____________ sales representatives can build dealer's enthusiasm by dramatizing plant advertising and sales promotion backup.
a) Increased stock position
b) Enthusiasm building
c) Missionary selling
d) Key account management
664. In __________ sales representatives can sign up more dealers.
a) Increased stock position
b) Enthusiasm building
c) Missionary selling
d) Key account management
665. In ____________ sales representatives can take responsibility for growing business with the most important account.

a) Increased stock position
b) Enthusiasm building
c) Missionary selling
d) Key account management

666. ___________ aims to create brand awareness and knowledge of new products or new features of existing products.
a) Informative advertising
b) Persuasive advertising
c) Reminder advertising
d) Reinforcement advertising

667. _____________ aims to create liking, preference, conviction and purchase of product or service.
a) Informative advertising
b) Persuasive advertising
c) Reminder advertising
d) Reinforcement advertising

668. ____________ aims to stimulate repeat purchase of products and services.
a) Informative advertising
b) Persuasive advertising
c) Reminder advertising
d) Reinforcement advertising

669. _______________ aims to convince current purchasers that they made the right choice.
a) Informative advertising
b) Persuasive advertising
c) Reminder advertising
d) Reinforcement advertising

670. The no. of repetitions needed to put across the brand's message to consumers that has an important impact on the advertising budget.
a) Advertising frequency
b) Product substitutability

c) Competition and clutter

d) Product life cycle

671. The no. of times with in the specific time period that an average person or household is exposed to the message is called

a) Reach

b) Frequency

c) Impact

d) Total no. of exposures

672. __________ is the qualitative value of an exposure through a given medium.

a) Reach

b) Frequency

c) Impact

d) Total no. of exposures

673. Total no. of exposures can be calculated as

a) Exposures = Reach * Frequency

b) Exposures = Reach * Impact

c) Exposures = Frequency * Impact

d) None of the above

674. Weighted no. of exposures is calculated as

a) Weighted exposure = Reach * Frequency * Impact

b) Weighted exposure = Reach * Frequency + Impact

c) Weighted exposure = Reach - Frequency * Impact

d) Weighted exposure = Reach + Frequency + Impact

675. Out of home advertising is also called as

a) Place advertising

b) Reminder advertising

c) Informative advertising

d) Logistics advertising

676. ____________ involves scheduling the advertising in a relation to seasons and the business cycle.

a) Microscheduling problem

b) Macroscheduling problem
c) Dominant influence
d) Pulsing

677. ____________ calls for allocating advertising expenditures within a short period to obtain maximum impact.
a) Microscheduling problem
b) Macroscheduling problem
c) Dominant influence
d) Pulsing

678. ____________ is achieved by scheduling exposures evenly throughout a given period.
a) Concentration
b) Continuity
c) Flighting
d) Pulsing

679. ____________ calls for spending the entire advertising amount in a single period.
a) Concentration
b) Continuity
c) Flighting
d) Pulsing

680. ____________ calls for advertising for a period, followed by a period with no advertising, followed by a second period of advertising activity.
a) Concentration
b) Continuity
c) Flighting
d) Pulsing

681. ____________ is continuous advertising at low weight levels reinforced periodically by waves of heavier activity.
a) Concentration
b) Continuity

c) Flighting
d) Pulsing

682. __________ seeks to determine whether an advertisement is communicating effectively.
a) Dominant influence
b) Cross promotions
c) Frequency
d) Communication effect research

683. Buying a greater quantity during the deal period than they can sell during the deal period is called:
a) Frequency programs
b) Forward buying
c) Backward buying
d) None of these

684. _____________consists of useful, low cost items bearing the company's name and address and sometimes an advertising message that salespeople give to prospects and customers.
a) Specialty advertising
b) Reminder advertising
c) Informative advertising
d) Logistics advertising

685. Dealing with legislators and government officials to promote or defeat legislation and regulation is called:
a) Lobbying
b) Marketing public relation
c) Publicity
d) Carpet bombing

686. The old name of marketing public relation was:
a) Sales promotion
b) Trade promotion
c) Publicity
d) Advertising

687. Direct mailers gather or buy as many names as possible and send out a mass mailing is called:
a) Database marketing
b) Interactive marketing
c) Carpet bombing
d) Lifetime value marketing
688. Direct marketers mine the database to identify prospects who would have the most interest in an offer is called:
a) Database marketing
b) Interactive marketing
c) Carpet bombing
d) Lifetime value marketing
689. Direct marketers include a telephone number and web address and offer to print coupons from website accounts to:
a) Database marketing
b) Interactive marketing
c) Carpet bombing
d) Lifetime value marketing
690. Direct marketers know enough about each customer to customize and personalize the offer and message is called:
a) Database marketing
b) Interactive marketing
c) Real time personalized marketing
d) Lifetime value marketing
691. Direct marketers develop a plan for lifetime marketing to each valuable customer, based on knowledge of life events and transitions is/ are called:
a) Database marketing
b) Interactive marketing
c) Carpet bombing
d) Lifetime value marketing
692. Telemarketing accounts to use of:

a) Emails
b) Text Message
c) Telephone
d) Transmission

693. In case of inbound telemarketing the marketer:
a) Receives calls from customers
b) Calls customers
c) Both a & b
d) None of these

694. In case of outbound telemarketing the marketer:
a) Receives calls from customers
b) Calls customers
c) Both a & b
d) None of these

695. Calling customers to maintain and nurture key account relationships and give more attention to neglected accounts is called:
a) Telesales
b) Telecoverage
c) Teleprospecting
d) Customer service

696. Generating and qualifying new leads for closure by another sales channel is called:
a) Telesales
b) Telecoverage
c) Teleprospecting
d) Customer service

697. A ____________is a limited area on the web managed and paid for by an external advertiser/company.
a) Sponsorship
b) Microsite
c) Interstitials
d) Content target advertising

698. ____________are advertisements, often with video or animation that pop up between changes on a web site.
a) Sponsorship
b) Microsite
c) Interstitials
d) Content target advertising
699. __________links ads not to keywords but to the content of web pages.
a) Sponsorship
b) Microsite
c) Interstitials
d) Content target advertising
700. A ____________is a salesperson who is not expected or permitted to take an order but whose major task is to build goodwill.
a) Demand creator
b) Solution vendor
c) Missionary
d) Both a & b
701. A salesperson that relies on creative methods for selling tangible products.
a) Order taker
b) Demand creator
c) Solution vendor
d) Deliverer
702. A salesperson whose expertise is in solving a customer's problem.
a) Order taker
b) Demand creator
c) Solution vendor
d) Deliverer
703. ___________includes resistance to interference and preference for established supply sources.
a) Psychological resistance

b) Logical resistance
c) Routinized exchange
d) Negotiated exchange

704. ____________might consists of objections to the price, delivery schedule or certain product or company characteristics.
a) Psychological resistance
b) Logical resistance
c) Routinized exchange
d) Negotiated exchange

705. In ____________the terms are established by administered programs of pricing and distribution.
a) Psychological resistance
b) Logical resistance
c) Routinized exchange
d) Negotiated exchange

706. In ___________price and other terms are set via bargaining behavior.
a) Psychological resistance
b) Logical resistance
c) Routinized exchange
d) Negotiated exchange

707. New products that create an entirely new market are called:
a) New product lines
b) New to the world products
c) Additions to existing product lines
d) Improvements and revisions of existing products

708. New products that allow a company to enter an established market for the first time are called:
a) New product lines
b) New to the world products
c) Additions to existing product lines
d) Improvements and revisions of existing products

709. Mew products that supplement established product lines are called:

a) New product lines
b) New to the world products
c) Additions to existing product lines
d) Improvements and revisions of existing products

710. New products that provide improved performance or grater perceived value and replace existing products is called:
a) New product lines
b) New to the world products
c) Additions to existing product lines
d) Improvements and revisions of existing products

711. Existing products that are targeted to new markets or market segments are called:
a) New product lines
b) Repositioning
c) Additions to existing product lines
d) Improvements and revisions of existing products

712. New products that provide similar performance at lower cost are called:
a) Cost reductions
b) Repositioning
c) Additions to existing product lines
d) Improvements and revisions of existing products

713. Companies have to aim their new products at smaller market segments and this can mean lower sales and profits for each product is called:
a) New product lines
b) Repositioning
c) Additions to existing product lines
d) Fragmented markets

714. ____________is a cross functional group charged with developing a

specific product or business.

a) Venture team

b) Functional team

c) Skunkworks

d) Stage gate system

715. ____________are informal workplaces where intrapreneurial teams attempt to develop new products.

a) Venture team

b) Functional team

c) Skunkworks

d) Stage gate system

716. ____________is the third state in new product development process:

a) Idea screening

b) Marketing strategy development

c) Concept development and testing

d) Product development

717. Which of the following is the fourth stage of new product development process:

a) Business Analysis

b) Marketing strategy development

c) Concept development and testing

d) Product development

718. Which of the following is the fifth stage of new product development process:

a) Business Analysis

b) Market testing

c) Concept development and testing

d) Product development

719. Which of the following is the sixth stage of new product development process:

a) Business Analysis

b) Market testing
c) Commercialization
d) Product development

720. Which of the following is the seventh stage of new product development process:
a) Business Analysis
b) Market testing
c) Commercialization
d) Product development

721. Which of the following is the eighth stage of new product development process:
a) Business Analysis
b) Market testing
c) Commercialization
d) Product development

722. Many firms use a ________________ that recognizes the value of returning to an earlier stage to make improvements before moving forward:
a) Funnel
b) Spiral development process
c) Mind mapping
d) Reverse assumption

723. ________lists the attributes of an object under creativity techniques.
a) Forced relationships
b) Morphological analysis
c) Reverse assumption
d) Attribute listing

724. __________starts with a problem under creativity techniques.
a) Forced relationships
b) Morphological analysis
c) Reverse assumption

d) Attribute listing

725. ___________starts with a thought under creativity techniques.

a) Forced relationships

b) Morphological analysis

c) Reverse assumption

d) Mind mapping

726. _________occurs when the company dismisses an otherwise good idea.

a) DROP error

b) Morphological analysis

c) Reverse assumption

d) Mind mapping

727. ___________occurs when the company permits a poor idea to move into development and commercialization.

a) DROP error

b) Go error

c) Partial product failure

d) Relative product failure

728. __________ loses money but its sales covers all its variable costs and some of its fixed costs.

a) DROP error

b) Go error

c) Partial product failure

d) Relative product failure

729. __________ yields a profit that is less than the company's target rate of return.

a) DROP error

b) Go error

c) Partial product failure

d) Relative product failure

730. _____________is the additional income on other company products resulting from adding this product to the line.

a) Dragalong income
b) Cannabalized income
c) Drawn income
d) None of these

731. ________is the reduced income on other company products resulting from adding this product to the line.
a) Dragalong income
b) Cannibalized income
c) Drawn income
d) None of these

732. ________is the name given to testing the product within the firm.
a) Alpha testing
b) Beta testing
c) Gama testing
d) Both a & c

733. ________enlists a set of customers to use the prototype and give feedback.
a) Alpha testing
b) Beta testing
c) Gama testing
d) Both a & c

734. ________method asks the consumer to rank the three items in order of preference.
a) Paired comparison
b) Monadic rating
c) Rank order
d) All the above

735. ________method calls for presenting pairs of items and asking the consumer which one is preferred in each pair.
a) Paired comparison
b) Monadic rating

c) Rank order
d) All the above

736. ________method asks the consumer to rate liking of each product on a scale.
a) Paired comparison
b) Monadic rating
c) Rank order
d) All the above

737. In__________ consumers who initially try the product at no cost are reoffered the product or a competitor's product at slightly reduced price.
a) Simulated test marketing
b) Controlled test marketing
c) Sales-Wave research
d) None of these

738. __________calls for finding 30 to 40 qualified shoppers and questioning them about brand familiarity and preferences in a specific product category.
a) Simulated test marketing
b) Controlled test marketing
c) Sales-Wave research
d) None of these

739. In __________ a research firm manages a panel of stores that will carry new products for a fee.
a) Simulated test marketing
b) Controlled test marketing
c) Sales-Wave research
d) None of these

740. In ________the firm time its entry to coincide with the competitor's entry in the market.
a) First order entry
b) Second order entry

c) Parallel entry

d) Above order entry

741. __________are technology enthusiasts and venturesome.

a) Innovators

b) Early adopters

c) Laggards

d) Early majority

742. __________ are opinion leaders who carefully search for new technologies.

a) Innovators

b) Early adopters

c) Laggards

d) Early majority

743. ___________are deliberate pragmatists.

a) Innovators

b) Early adopters

c) Laggards

d) Early majority

744. ___________are skeptical conservatives.

a) Late majority

b) Early adopters

c) Laggards

d) Early majority

745. __________are traditional bound people and resist innovation until they find that the status quo is no longer defensible.

a) Innovators

b) Early adopters

c) Laggards

d) Early majority

746. In general there are ____________ characteristics of innovation.

a) Three

b) Four

c) Five
d) Six
747. ________is the degree to which the innovation appears superior to existing products.
a) Compatibility
b) Relative advantage
c) Complexity
d) Divisibility
748. ________is the degree to which the innovation matches the values and experiences of the individuals.
a) Compatibility
b) Relative advantage
c) Complexity
d) Divisibility
749. ________is the degree to which the innovation is relatively difficult to understand or use.
a) Compatibility
b) Relative advantage
c) Complexity
d) Divisibility
750. ________is the degree to which innovation can be tried on a limited basis.
a) Compatibility
b) Relative advantage
c) Complexity
d) Divisibility
751. ________is the degree to which the beneficial results of use are observable or describable to others.
a) Compatibility
b) Relative advantage
c) Communicability
d) Divisibility

752. The internationalization process has __________stages.

a) Four

b) Five

c) Six

d) Three

753. In__________countries are gradually entered sequentially.

a) Relative advantage

b) Waterfall approach

c) Sprinkler approach

d) Both b & c

754. In__________countries are entered simultaneously.

a) Relative advantage

b) Waterfall approach

c) Sprinkler approach

d) Both b & c

755. NAFTA stands for:

a) North American Free Trade Agreement

b) North American Free Trade Association

c) North African Free Trade Agreement

d) North African Free Trade Association

756. APEC stands for:

a) American Pacific Economic Cooperation

b) African Pacific Economic Cooperation

c) Asian Pacific Economic Cooperation

d) None of these

757. __________represents a passive level of involvement in which the company exports from time to time either on its own initiative or in response to unsolicited orders from abroad.

a) Occasional exporting

b) Active exporting

c) Indirect exporting

d) Domestic based exporting

758. ________takes place when a company makes a commitment to expand into a particular market.

a) Occasional exporting
b) Active exporting
c) Indirect exporting
d) Domestic based exporting

759. In________ companies work through independent intermediaries.

a) Occasional exporting
b) Active exporting
c) Indirect exporting
d) Domestic based exporting

760. In ____________the firm hires local manufacturers to produce the product.

a) Management contracts
b) Contract manufacturing
c) Joint venture
d) Franchising

761. ________means introducing the product in the foreign market without any change.

a) Straight extension
b) Product adoption
c) Reengineering
d) Forward innovation

762. ________involves altering the product to meet local conditions or preferences.

a) Straight extension
b) Product adaptation
c) Reengineering
d) Forward innovation

763. ________represents reintroducing earlier product forms that are well adapted to a foreign country's needs.

a) Product invention
b) Backward invention
c) Forward invention
d) Communication adaptation

764. __________is creating a new product to meet a need in another country.

a) Product invention
b) Backward invention
c) Forward invention
d) Communication adaptation

765. ________occurs when a company charges either less than its costs or less than it charges in its home market.

a) Gray market
b) Arm's length price
c) Dumping
d) Transfer price

766. __________is the price charged by other competitors for the same or similar product.

a) Gray market
b) Arm's length price
c) Dumping
d) Transfer price

767. ________consists of branded products diverted from normal or authorized distribution channels in the country of product origin.

a) Gray market
b) Arm's length price
c) Dumping
d) Transfer price

768. __________represents appointing teams to manage customer value building processes and break down walls between departments.

a) Outsourcing
b) Benchmarking

c) Flattening

d) Reengineering

769. ________represents studying best practice companies to improve performance.

a) Outsourcing

b) Benchmarking

c) Flattening

d) Reengineering

770. __________represents reducing the number of organizational levels to get closer to the customer.

a) Outsourcing

b) Benchmarking

c) Flattening

d) Reengineering

771. BAMT stands for

a) Brand Assessment Management Team

b) Brand Asset Management Team

c) Brand Assessment Management Terminal

d) Brand Asset Management Terminal

772. ___________is the marketing that links the firm's contributions to a designated cause to customers.

a) Corporate societal marketing

b) Cause related marketing

c) Social marketing

d) Societal marketing

773. Cause marketing is also called a part of:

a) Corporate societal marketing

b) Cause related marketing

c) Social marketing

d) Societal marketing

774. In ___________pattern a firm creates own cause programme.

a) Co-branded

b) Self-branded
c) Jointly branded
d) None of these

775. In ______________ pattern a firm has a link to existing cause program.
a) Co-branded
b) Self-branded
c) Jointly branded
d) None of these

776. In __________ the firms partner with an existing cause but explicitly brand the program that links to the cause.
a) Co-branded
b) Self-branded
c) Jointly branded
d) None of these

777. __________is done by a non-profit organization or government.
a) Corporate societal marketing
b) Cause related marketing
c) Social marketing
d) Societal marketing

778. "Motivate people to donate blood" is associated with:
a) Behavioural campaign
b) Value campaign
c) Action campaign
d) Both b & c

779. "Demotivate cigarette smoking" is associated with:
a) Behavioural campaign
b) Value campaign
c) Action campaign
d) None of these

780. "Motivate women to take pap test" is associated with:
a) Behavioural campaign

b) Value campaign
c) Action campaign
d) None of these
781. "Alter ideas about abortion" is associated with:
a) Behavioural campaign
b) Value campaign
c) Action campaign
d) None of these
782. ____________are small, rectangular boxes containing text and perhaps a picture to support a brand.
a) Advertising
b) Publicity
c) Banner Ads
d) Hoardings
783. __________are the products that are necessary to the use of other products.
a) Captive products
b) Secondary products
c) Derived products
d) None of these
784. In __________producers sell their products to dealers only if they purchase related products as well.
a) Vertical Marketing
b) Horizontal Marketing
c) Tying Agreement
d) Value Delivery System
785. ____________is the rate at which the buyer forgets the brand.
a) Declining rate
b) Forgetting rate
c) Overlook rate
d) Negative rate
786. ___________is a set of procedures and sources managers use to ob-

tain everyday information about developments in the marketing environment.
a) Marketing Intelligence System
b) Management Intelligence System
c) Business Intelligence System
d) Marketing Information System
787. RTA stands for:
a) Ready to access
b) Ready to assemble
c) Ready to admittance
d) None of these
788. __________ values and beliefs are not open to change.
a) Core
b) Secondary
c) Both a & b
d) None of these
789. __________ values and beliefs are open to change.
a) Core
b) Secondary
c) Both a & b
d) None of these
790. MDSS stands for:
a) Management decision support system
b) Marketing decision support system
c) Manufacturing decision support system
d) Multipurpose decision support system
791. __________refers to bringing the products at important and convenient places.
a) Concentration
b) Equalization
c) Dispersion
d) Possession utility

792. __________is the process by means of which the supply of goods is adjusted in accordance with their demand.
a) Concentration
b) Equalization
c) Dispersion
d) Possession utility
793. __________refers to distribution of goods which are concentrated to the final customers.
a) Concentration
b) Equalization
c) Dispersion
d) Possession utility
794. _________is created by storing products produced in godowns till then they are consumed.
a) Time utility
b) Place utility
c) Possession utility
d) All the above
795. _________is created by transporting goods produced from the place of production to the place of consumption.
a) Time utility
b) Place utility
c) Possession utility
d) None of these
796. _________is created by transferring ownership.
a) Time utility
b) Place utility
c) Possession utility
d) All the above
797. Which of the following explained marketing functions as a major specialized activity?
a) Clark and Clark

b) Mc Carty

c) Proper Pyle

d) Harry L. Hensen

798. Mc Carty defined __________ marketing functions.

a) Five

b) Six

c) Seven

d) Nine

799. Who among the following provided two fold classification of marketing functions?

a) Clark and Clark

b) Mc Carty

c) Proper Pyle

d) Harry L. Hensen

800. Who among the following provided classification of marketing functions in two groups?

a) Clark and Clark

b) Mc Carty

c) Proper Pyle

d) Harry L. Hensen

801. In ____________ each member of the population has an equal chance of selection.

a) Simple random sample

b) Stratified random sample

c) Cluster sample

d) Convenience sample

802. In ____________ the population is divided into mutually exclusive groups and random samples are drawn from each group.

a) Simple random sample

b) Stratified random sample

c) Cluster sample

d) Convenience sample

803. In __________ the population is divided into mutually exclusive groups and the researcher draws a sample of the groups to interview.
a) Simple random sample
b) Stratified random sample
c) Cluster sample
d) Convenience sample
804. In __________the researcher selects the most accessible population members.
a) Simple random sample
b) Stratified random sample
c) Cluster sample
d) Convenience sample
805. In__________ the researcher selects population members who are good prospects for accurate information.
a) Simple random sample
b) Judgment sample
c) Cluster sample
d) Convenience sample
806. In__________ the researcher finds and interviews a prescribed number of people in each of several categories.
a) Simple random sample
b) Quota sample
c) Cluster sample
d) Convenience sample
807. In __________ respondents are contacted for an appointment and often a small payment or incentive is offered.
a) Personal interview
b) Arranged interview
c) Intercept interview
d) Telephone interview
808. In financial analysis of a product, the return on net worth is the product of__________ratios.

a) Two
b) Three
c) Four
d) One
809. In financial analysis of a product, the return on net worth is the product of two ratios. These are:
a) Return on assets & financial leverage
b) Net assets & financial leverage
c) Net profit and financial leverage
d) Net profit and marketing operating expenses
810. Asset turnover =
a) Net sales/Total assets
b) Net profits/Total assets
c) Total assets/Net worth
d) Net profits/Net worth
811. Return on assets:
a) Net sales/Total assets
b) Net profits/Total assets
c) Total assets/Net worth
d) Net profits/Net worth
812. Financial leverage:
a) Net sales/Total assets
b) Net profits/Total assets
c) Total assets/Net worth
d) Net profits/Net worth
813. Rate of return on net worth:
a) Net sales/Total assets
b) Net profits/Total assets
c) Total assets/Net worth
d) Net profits/Net worth
814. __________are the costs that can be assigned only indirectly but on a plausible basis.

a) Direct costs
b) Traceable common costs
c) Nontraceable common costs
d) Sunk costs

815. ___________are the costs whose allocation to the marketing entities is highly arbitrary.
a) Direct costs
b) Traceable common costs
c) Nontraceable common costs
d) Sunk costs

816. The eligible adults constitute the _________market.
a) Potential market
b) Available market
c) Target market
d) Qualified available market

817. The distance between the market minimum and the market potential shows the overall_____________.
a) Expansible market
b) Nonexpansible market
c) Marketing sensitivity of demand
d) Expansible market

818. _______ market is very much affected in its total size by the level of industry marketing expenditure.
a) Expansible market
b) Nonexpansible market
c) Marketing sensitivity of demand
d) Expansible market

819. _______ market is not affected by the level of industry marketing expenditure.
a) Expansible market
b) Nonexpansible market
c) Marketing sensitivity of demand

d) Expansible market

820. The experts exchange views and produce a group estimate is called:

a) Group discussion method

b) Pooling of individual estimates

c) Delphi method

d) Exponential smoothing

821. The experts supply their estimates individually and an analyst combines them into a single estimate is called:

a) Group discussion method

b) Pooling of individual estimates

c) Delphi method

d) Exponential smoothing

822. The experts supply individual estimates and assumptions and the firm analyzes and revises them is called:

a) Group discussion method

b) Pooling of individual estimates

c) Delphi method

d) Exponential smoothing

823. ________is the bundle of costs customers expect to incur in evaluating, obtaining, using and disposing of a given market offering.

a) Total customer cost

b) Total fixed cost

c) Total variable cost

d) Psychic cost

824. ______________is a person's feeling of pleasure or disappointment resulting from comparing a product's perceived performance.

a) Satisfaction

b) Attitude

c) Behavior

d) Perception

825. CPA stands for:

a) Company profitability analysis
b) Customer profitability analysis
c) Consumer profitability analysis
d) Corporate profitability analysis

826. ABC stands for:
a) Activity based costing
b) Action based costing
c) Activity based controlling
d) Action based controlling

827. "Customers for Life" have been written by:
a) Sewell and Brown
b) Brown and Pamela
c) Sewell and George
d) Belch and Irwin

828. _________is the total of the discounted lifetime values of all the firm's customers.
a) Brand equity
b) Value equity
c) Relationship equity
d) Customer equity

829. _________is the company's ability to perform in one or more ways that competitors cannot match.
a) Competitive advantage
b) Leverageable advantage
c) Comparative advantage
d) Customer advantage

830. _________is the cumulative value of the firm's network of relationships with its customers, partners, suppliers, employees and investors.
a) Brand equity
b) Value equity
c) Relational equity
d) Customer equity

831. A ___________ is any occasion on which a customer encounters the brand and product.

a) Customer relationship management

b) Partner relationship management

c) Customer touch point

d) Customer equity

832. High customer churn is also called as:

a) High customer defection

b) High customer evaluation

c) High customer involvement

d) None of these

833. Through ___________ the marketing statisticians can extract useful information about individuals, trends and segments from the mass of data.

a) Data warehouse

b) Datamining

c) Data extraction

d) Database marketing

834. The needs that arise from physiological states are called:

a) Psychogenic needs

b) Biogenic needs

c) Motives

d) Self-realization

835. Who among the following assumed that psychological forces shaping people's behavior are largely unconscious?

a) Sigmund Freud

b) Frederick Herzberg

c) Abraham Maslow

d) Michael Belch

836. ___________ needs arise from psychological states of tension.

a) Psychogenic needs

b) Biogenic needs

c) Motives

d) Self-realization

837. ____________can be used to trace a person's motivations.

a) Laddering

b) Psychogenic needs

c) Biogenic needs

d) Perception

838. ___________is the process by which a person selects organizes and interprets information to give meaning to environment.

a) Personality

b) Motivation

c) Reinforcement

d) Perception

839. __________means that marketer have to work hard to attract consumers.

a) Selective distortion

b) Subliminal perception

c) Selective attention

d) Selective retention

840. ____________involves permanent changes in the individual behavior arising from experience.

a) Personality

b) Learning

c) Reinforcement

d) Perception

841. _________represents all the brands available to the consumer.

a) Awareness set

b) Total set

c) Consideration set

d) None of these

842. _________represents a consumer shall come to know about these brands.

a) Awareness set
b) Total set
c) Consideration set
d) Choice set

843. ________represents that some brands shall meet the initial buying criteria.
a) Awareness set
b) Total set
c) Consideration set
d) Choice set

844. As the consumer gathers more information, only a few will remain as strong contender brands are known as:
a) Awareness set
b) Total set
c) Consideration set
d) Choice set

845. ________is an evaluation of favorable or unfavorable feelings and emotions.
a) Behavior
b) Attitude
c) Motivation
d) Referent power

846. Expectancy value model is also called a:
a) Noncompensatory model
b) Compensatory model
c) Behavioural model
d) Motivation theory

847. Solution selling can also alleviate:
a) Cost
b) Quality
c) Price
d) Promotion

848. Specialized Web sites are also called as:
a) Catalog sites
b) Auction sites
c) E-hubs
d) E-commerce
849. Marketing to smaller segments and niches is called:
a) Segment marketing
b) Focus
c) Micromarketing
d) Skimming marketing
850. PRIZM has been developed by:
a) Microsoft corp.
b) IBM
c) Claritas Inc.
d) INTEL
851. ___________means a consumer is willing to pay a little more for convenience.
a) Innovation opportunity
b) Packaging
c) Consumer affluence
d) Hybrid
852. In__________ the company asks consumers what benefits they would like to be added to the product and their desire level for each.
a) Customer survey process
b) Intuitive process
c) Dialectical process
d) Needs-hierarchy process
853. In __________entrepreneurs get hunches and undertake product development without much marketing research.
a) Customer survey process
b) Intuitive process
c) Dialectical process

d) Needs-hierarchy process

854. In ________innovators should not march with the crowd.

a) Customer survey process

b) Intuitive process

c) Dialectical process

d) Needs-hierarchy process

855. In __________the innovators task is to assess when the market is ready to satisfy a higher order need.

a) Customer survey process

b) Intuitive process

c) Dialectical process

d) Needs-hierarchy process

856. In PRIZM there are ________broad categories.

a) Five

b) Six

c) Seven

d) Eleven

857. In PRIZM there are ________ factors.

a) Thirty five

b) Thirty seven

c) Thirty nine

d) Forty three

858. People play ___________roles in buying decision.

a) Four

b) Five

c) Six

d) Seven

859. ________have been developed to measure the strength of the psychological commitment between brands and consumers and their openness to change.

a) Psychological Segmentation

b) Psychological Positioning

c) Behavioural Model
d) Conversion Model
860. ________is the strategic coordination of economic, psychological, political and public relations skill to gain the cooperation of number of parties.
a) Stratified marketing
b) Holistic marketing
c) Mega marketing
d) Societal marketing
861. In ____________ the buyer first decides the manufacturer and then its product/brand.
a) Brand dominant strategy
b) Region dominant strategy
c) Nation dominant strategy
d) Industry dominant strategy
862. In ____________ the buyer first decides the nation and then product/brand.
a) Brand dominant strategy
b) Region dominant strategy
c) Nation dominant strategy
d) Industry dominant strategy
863. BAV stands for:
a) Brand Asset Valuation
b) Brand Asset Valuator
c) Brand Asset Volatility
d) None of these
864. BAV model was developed by:
a) Young and Rubicam
b) Standard and Poor
c) NIKKI
d) ONIDA
865. According to BAV model there are _______pillars of brand equity.

a) Two
b) Three
c) Four
d) Five

866. _______means when a firm takes longer time to respond to marketing crisis, consumers form negative impressions about the firm.
a) Sincere
b) Swiftness
c) Aggression
d) Recapitalization

867. Individual family names and blanket family names are sometimes called:
a) House of brands
b) Brand extension
c) Brand revitalization
d) Brand reinforcement

868. ___________can be difficult and often requires sub-branding strategies.
a) Horizontal extensions
b) Vertical extensions
c) Both a & b
d) None of these

869. _________ pattern represents characteristics of small kitchen appliances.
a) Growth-slum maturity
b) Cycle-recycle
c) Scalloped
d) U-shaped

870. _________ pattern represents sales of new drugs.
a) Growth-slum maturity
b) Cycle-recycle

c) Scalloped
d) U-shaped
871. In ____________ pattern sale passes through a succession of life cycles based on the discovery of new product characteristics.
a) Growth-slum maturity
b) Cycle-recycle
c) Scalloped
d) U-shaped
872. The first to develop patents in new product category is called:
a) Innovator
b) Inventor
c) Product pioneer
d) Market pioneer
873. The first to develop a working model is called:
a) Innovator
b) Inventor
c) Product pioneer
d) Market pioneer
874. The first to sell in new product category is called:
a) Innovator
b) Inventor
c) Product pioneer
d) Market pioneer
875. ________aim at increasing the product's esthetic appeal.
a) Style
b) Style improvements
c) Style mobilization
d) Inventions
876. __________calls for gradually reducing a product or business costs while trying to maintain sale.
a) Divestment
b) Disinvestment

c) Harvesting
d) Retrenchment
877. Threat of mobility comes from:
a) Suppliers
b) Substitutes
c) Buyers
d) Potential entrants
878. Producing high quality equipment's known for its reliability and durability is called:
a) Premium performance
b) Efficient dealership system
c) Superior service
d) Full line strategy
879. ______________maintains the largest number of independent equipment dealers in the industry.
a) Premium performance
b) Extensive and efficient dealership system
c) Superior service
d) Full line strategy
880. Adam Morgan offered __________ suggestions to how small brands can compete in a better way.
a) Five
b) Six
c) Seven
d) Eight
881. _________is the totality of features that affect how a product looks and functions in terms of customer requirement.
a) Blueprint
b) Design
c) Manufacturing
d) Supply Chain
882. QRS stands for:

a) Quality Resource System
b) Quick Response System
c) Query Response System
d) None of these
883. GPS stands for:
a) Global Positioning System
b) General Positioning System
c) Global Positioning Software
d) Both a & b
884. ____________consists of a fixed fee plus a variable usage fee.
a) By product pricing
b) Two part pricing
c) Mixed bundling
d) Pure bundling
885. Co-branding is also known as:
a) Dual branding
b) Brand bundling
c) Both a & b
d) None of the above
886. In ______________the two retail establishments use the same location as a way to optimize both space and profit.
a) Dual branding
b) Brand bundling
c) Retail co-branding
d) Same company co-branding
887. A pictorial representation of various clues is called:
a) Experience blueprint
b) Context clues
c) Credence qualities
d) None of these
888. The statement "How the respondents should be chosen?" comes under:

a) Sampling Unit
b) Sample Size
c) Sampling Procedure
d) Random Sample

889. ___________will shift some demand from peak to off peak periods.

a) Variability
b) Perishability
c) Differential pricing
d) Skimming pricing

890. The statement "Was the surgery successful" accounts to:

a) Conformance quality
b) Technical quality
c) Functional quality
d) Internal quality

891. The statement "Did the surgeon show concern and inspire confidence?" accounts to:

a) Conformance quality
b) Technical quality
c) Functional quality
d) Internal quality

892. In ___________suppliers create better information systems and in other ways help customers.

a) Reliability
b) Resilience
c) Innovativeness
d) Customer service

893. SSTS stands for:

a) Self-service technologies
b) Social service technologies
c) Sustainable service technological system
d) Either a or b

894. Zeithaml, Parasuraman& Malhotra identified ___________dimensions of e-service quality.
a) Ten
b) Eleven
c) Thirteen
d) Fourteen
895. Wolfinbarger and Gilly developed ___________ dimensions of online service quality.
a) Six
b) Five
c) Four
d) Three
896. _________is used to probe customer satisfiers or dissatisfiers.
a) Voice of the customer
b) Resilience
c) Innovativeness
d) Reliability
897. VOC stands for:
a) Voice of the customer
b) Value on counter
c) Voice of corporates
d) Either b or c
898. Service contracts are also known as:
a) Warranties
b) Guarantees
c) Extended warranties
d) Extended guarantees
899. _________pricing is effective with ego-sensitive products.
a) Psychological
b) Image
c) Competition
d) Value

900. The manufacturer's unit cost =

a) Variable cost + Fixed cost/Unit sales

b) Fixed cost + Variable cost/Unit sales

c) Variable cost- Fixed cost/Unit sales

d) Fixed cost-Variable cost/Unit sales

901. Markup price =

a) Unit cost/1-desired return on sales

b) Unit cost-1/desired return on sales

c) Unit cost/1+desired return on sales

d) None of these

902. Target return price =

a) Unit cost + desired return*invested capital/unit sales

b) Unit cost + desired return*invested capital

c) Unit cost- desired return*invested capital/unit sale

d) None of these

903. Break even volume =

a) Fixed cost/price-variable cost

b) Variable cost/price-fixed cost

c) Fixed cost-price/variable cost

d) Either b or c

904. Higher level of management should conduct a__________ to arrive at the real price of their offering.

a) Price analysis

b) Net price analysis

c) Gross price analysis

d) Inflation

905. ________buy, take title and resell the merchandise.

a) Agents

b) Facilitators

c) Merchants

d) Wholesalers

906. __________ search for customers, negotiate on producers behalf

but do not take title of goods.

a) Agents

b) Facilitators

c) Merchants

d) Wholesalers

907. __________assist in the distribution process but neither take title to goods not negotiate sales.

a) Agents

b) Facilitators

c) Merchants

d) Wholesalers

908. _____________is a system of partnerships and alliances that a firm creates to source, augment and deliver its offerings.

a) Value network

b) Augmented network

c) Channel network

d) All the above

909. In _____________the producer hopes to obtain more dedicated and knowledgeable selling.

a) Selective distribution

b) Intensive distribution

c) Exclusive distribution

d) Exclusive dealing

910. _____________refers to payment terms and producer guarantees.

a) Conditions of sale

b) Selective distribution

c) Agreement to sell

d) Selling conditions

911. The traditional system is the

a) Manufacturer sponsored wholesaler franchise

b) Manufacturer sponsored retailer franchise

c) Service firm sponsored retailer franchise

d) All of the above

912. The term market is obtained from Latin word

a) Marcatus

b) Marcat

c) Catus

d) Orchad

913. "Marketing is the business process by which products are matched with markets and through which transfers of ownerships are effected," was quoted by

a) Cundiff and Still

b) Converse and Mitchell

c) Duddy and Reizan

d) Hopper Harry

914. "Marketing is an integrating system of action that creates value in goods through the creation of form, place, time and ownership utilities," was marked by

a) Buskirk Richard

b) Converse and Mitchell

c) Duddy and Reizan

d) Hopper Harry

915. "Marketing is the process of getting the right goods to the right consumers at the right place and time and at the right price", was said by

a) Cundiff and Still

b) Converse and Mitchell

c) M. Banerjee

d) Hopper Harry

916. "Marketing is getting and keeping the customer" was remarked by:

a) Theodore Levitt

b) Converse and Mitchell

c) Duddy and Reizan

d) Hopper Harry

917. "Marketing is that phase of business activity through which human wants are satisfied by exchange of goods and services" was marked by:

a) Cundiff and Still

b) J.F. Pyle

c) Duddy and Reizan

d) Hopper Harry

918. "Marketing is the creation and delivery of a standard of living" was given by

a) Cundiff and Still

b) Converse and Mitchell

c) Duddy and Reizan

d) Malcolm McNair

919. "Marketing management is directly concerned with the direction of purposeful activities toward the attainment of marketing goods" was said by:

a) Cundiff and Still

b) Converse and Mitchell

c) Duddy and Reizan

d) Hopper Harry

920. "Marketing management is that filed of business activity involving the establishment and execution of the plans of all the phases or steps of a complete sales campaign"

a) L. K. Johnson

b) Converse and Mitchell

c) Duddy and Reizan

d) Hopper Harry

921. "Grading involves the division of products into classes made up of units possessing similar characteristics of size and quality" was said by:

a) F. F. Clark

b) Converse and Mitchell

c) Duddy and Reizan

d) Hopper Harry

922. __________is also known as scattered buying.

a) Diversified buying

b) Reciprocal buying

c) Conservative buying

d) Speculative buying

923. Under which practice of buying, buyers and sellers buy and sell their products to each other.

a) Diversified buying

b) Reciprocal buying

c) Conservative buying

d) Speculative buying

924. In___________ buying goods are purchased in bulk quantity to sell them at higher prices in near future.

a) Diversified buying

b) Reciprocal buying

c) Conservative buying

d) Speculative buying

925. ___________is based on the current needs of buyer. Goods are frequently purchased by the buyer in small quantity.

a) Diversified buying

b) Reciprocal buying

c) Conservative buying

d) Speculative buying

926. "Marketing planning is the exercise of analysis and foresight to increase the effectiveness of marketing activities" is said by:

a) McDonald Malcolm

b) Wendell Smith

c) Duddy and Reizan

d) Hopper Harry

927. The term Marketing Mix was introduced by:

a) McDonald Malcolm

b) Wendell Smith
c) Duddy and Reizan
d) Neil H. Borden

928. "Product is a bundle of utilities consisting of various product features and accompanying services".
a) McDonald Malcolm
b) W. J. Stanton
c) Harry L. Hanson
d) W. Alderson

929. __________ is the act of putting a limit on the number of varieties of a product.
a) Product innovation
b) Product diversification
c) Product standardization
d) Product elimination

930. ____________________ refers to withdraw a non-profitable product from the market.
a) Product innovation
b) Product diversification
c) Product standardization
d) Product elimination

931. "Packaging is the embracing functions of package selection manufacture, filling and handling" was quoted by:
a) D. Schwartz
b) Philip Kotler
c) Indian Institute of Packaging
d) W. Stanton

932. "Packaging is the general group of activities in designing the containers or wrappers for the products" was quoted by:
a) D. Schwartz
b) Philip Kotler
c) Indian Institute of Packaging

d) W. Stanton

933. Expected profit =

a) Total cash inflows - (Expected output*Cost per unit)

b) Total cash inflows +(Expected output*Cost per unit)

c) Total cash inflows / (Expected output*Cost per unit)

d) Total cash inflows - (Expected output+ Cost per unit)

934. "A set of independent organizations involved in the process of making a product or service available for use or consumption", was remarked by

a) American Marketing Association

b) D. A. Reuzan

c) Cundiff

d) Philip Kotler

935. "Mail order business is a retail organization that receives the supply order by mail and sell the goods by mail", was stated by

a) American Marketing Association

b) D. A. Reuzan

c) Cundiff

d) Asplay and Harknese

936. "Chain stores is a group of stores handling similar lines of merchandise with single ownership and centralized location", was said by

a) P. D. Converse

b) P. H. Nystrom

c) J. L. Fri

d) M. Zimmerman

937. "Advertising is mass communication of information intended to persuade buyers so as to maximize profit", was said by

a) P. D. Converse

b) P. H. Nystrom

c) J. L. Fri

d) Littlefield and Krikpatrick

938. "Advertising is to give public notice or to announce publicity" was

quoted by
a) Dr. Jones
b) American Marketing Association
c) Webster
d) Roland
939. “Advertising is selling in print or presenting a commodity in print to the people in such a way that they may be induced to buy it”, was stated by
a) Dr. Jones
b) Prof. Starch
c) Webster
d) Roland
940. “Advertising nourishes the consuming power of man and creates wants for better standard of living”, was said by
a) Dr. Jones
b) American Marketing Association
c) Churchil
d) Roland
941. “Sales promotion is the achievement of short term marketing objectives by schematic means” was said by
a) American Marketing Association
b) L. K. Johnson
c) W. J. Stanton
d) Christian Peterson
942. “Personnel selling involves oral presentation in a conversation with one or more prospective purchases for the purpose of making sales” was said by
a) Philip Kotler
b) Cundiff
c) American Marketing Association
d) Russel
943. “Personnel selling is an attempt to induce people to buy goods” was

remarked by
a) Philip Kotler
b) Cundiff
c) American Marketing Association
d) W. G. Carter
944. "Service is an activity offered for sale which yields benefits and satisfactions without leading to a physical change in the form of good" was said by
a) Gronross
b) K. J. Balois
c) Philip Kotler
d) Brian Norris
945. "Service or deeds, processes and performances" was remarked by
a) Zeithmal and Bitner
b) K. J. Balois
c) Philip Kotler
d) Brian Norris
946. "Goods are produced, sold and then consumed whereas the services are sold and then produced and consumed" was quoted by
a) Gronross
b) Donald Cowell
c) Philip Kotler
d) Brian Norris
947. The first classification of services was given by
a) Gronross
b) K. J. Balois
c) Robert Judd
d) Brian Norris
948. The first classification of services was given in
a) 1963
b) 1964
c) 1965

d) 1966

949. There are as many as ______________ classifications of services.

a) 12

b) 15

c) 18

d) 21

950. American Marketing Association was one of the pioneer in defining the term services in

a) 1960

b) 1961

c) 1963

d) 1965

951. The article "The Service Revolution" has been written by:

a) W.J. Rajan

b) J.M. Rathmell

c) K.J. Blois

d) William J. Stanton

952. The article "The Service Revolution" has been written by W.J. Rajan in:

a) 1961

b) 1962

c) 1963

d) 1964

953. The article "The Case of Redefining Services" has been written by:

a) W.J. Rajan

b) Robert C. Judd

c) K.J. Blois

d) William J. Stanton

954. The article "The Case of Redefining Services" has been written in:

a) 1962

b) 1963

c) 1964
d) 1965
955. The book "Marketing in the Service Sector" has been written by:
a) W.J. Rajan
b) J.M. Rathmell
c) K.J. Blois
d) William J. Stanton
956. The book "Marketing in the Service Sector" has been written in:
a) 1974
b) 1975
c) 1976
d) 1977
957. The article "Unique aspects of marketing of services" is written by:

a) W.J. Rajan
b) R.M. Bessorn
c) K.J. Blois
d) William J. Stanton
958. The article "Unique aspects of marketing of services" is written in:
a) 1974
b) 1975
c) 1976
d) 1978
959. The article "The Marketing of Services" is written by:
a) K.J. Blois
b) W. J. Stanton
c) J. Lehtinen
d) Philip Kotler
960. The book "Fundamentals of Marketing" is written by:
a) K.J. Blois
b) W. J. Stanton
c) J. Lehtinen

d) Philip Kotler

961. The book "Consumer Oriented Firm" is written by:

a) K.J. Blois

b) W. J. Stanton

c) J. Lehtinen

d) Philip Kotler

962. The book "Consumer Oriented Firm" is written in:

a) 1980

b) 1983

c) 1986

d) 1989

963. The book "Marketing of Professional Services" is written by:

a) K.J. Blois & W. J. Stanton

b) W. J. Stanton & J. Lehtinen

c) J. Lehtinen& Philip Kotler

d) Philip Kotler & Paul N. Bloom

964. The book "Marketing of Professional Services" is written in:

a) 1980

b) 1984

c) 1986

d) 1989

965. The book "Service Management and Marketing" is written by:

a) K.J. Blois

b) W. J. Stanton

c) C. Gronross

d) Philip Kotler

966. The book "Service Management and Marketing" is written in:

a) 1988

b) 1989

c) 1990

d) 1992

967. "Marketing mix is the pack of four sets of variables namely, prod-

uct variables, price variables, promotion variables and place variables" is quoted by:
a) Philip Kotler
b) J. McArthy
c) American Marketing Association
d) C. Gronross
968. "Marketing mix is the set of the marketing tools that the firm uses to pursue its marketing objectives in the target market" is quoted by:
a) Philip Kotler
b) J. McArthy
c) American Marketing Association
d) C. Gronross
969. E-Marketing is also known as:
a) Digital Marketing
b) Search Marketing
c) Web Marketing
d) All the above
970. "Green marketing is the marketing of products that are presumed to be environmentally safe" is quoted by:
a) Philip Kotler
b) J. McArthy
c) American Marketing Association
d) C. Gronross
971. "Ambush marketing is the marketing strategy in which a competing brand connects itself with a major sporting event with paying sponsorship fee" is quoted by:
a) Philip Kotler
b) J. McArthy
c) Macmillan
d) McCarthy
972. The term "ambush marketing" was introduced by:
a) Philip Kotler

b) Jerry Walsh
c) Macmillan
d) McCarthy

973. __________refers to intentional false claims to official sponsorship by a non-sponsor.
a) Coattail ambushing
b) Predatory ambushing
c) Ambushing by association
d) Value-based ambushing

974. __________is an attempt made by a brand to directly associate itself with a property or event by playing up a connection to the property that is legitimate but does not involve financial sponsorship.
a) Coattail ambushing
b) Predatory ambushing
c) Ambushing by association
d) Value-based ambushing

975. __________is the use of imagery or terminology not protected by intellectual property laws to create an illusion than a company has links to a sporting event or property.
a) Coattail ambushing
b) Predatory ambushing
c) Ambushing by association
d) Value-based ambushing

976. Total market logistics cost =
a) Total freight cost - Total fixed warehouse cost + Total variable warehouse costs + Total cost of lost sales due to average delivery delay.
b) Total freight cost + Total fixed warehouse cost + Total variable warehouse costs + Total cost of lost sales due to average delivery delay.
c) Total freight cost + Total fixed warehouse cost + Total variable warehouse costs
d) Total freight cost + Total variable warehouse costs + Total cost of lost sales due to average delivery delay.

977. ___________store goods for moderate to long periods of time.

a) Distribution warehouses

b) Automated warehouses

c) Storage warehouses

d) None of these

978. _____________receives goods from various company plants and suppliers and move them out as soon as possible.

a) Distribution warehouses

b) Automated warehouses

c) Storage warehouses

d) None of these

979. _________employ strong and advanced materials handling systems under the control of a central computer.

a) Distribution warehouses

b) Automated warehouses

c) Storage warehouses

d) None of these

980. ______________consists of setup costs and running costs.

a) Order processing costs

b) Opportunity costs

c) Inventory carrying costs

d) Variable costs

981. Order processing costs must be compared with ___________.

a) Order processing costs

b) Opportunity costs

c) Inventory carrying costs

d) Variable costs

982. In ____________target audience might prefer a particular product but not develop an opinion about buying it.

a) Awareness

b) Conviction

c) Knowledge

d) Product attitude

983. Who said this "Attitude change will take place in the direction of increasing the amount of congruity between the two evaluations.

a) Irving & Kotler

b) Gladwell & Irving

c) Osgood & Tannenbaum

d) Noreen & Jennifer

984. ________consists of company sales people contacting buyers in the target market.

a) Expert channels

b) Advocate channels

c) Social channels

d) Delivery channels

985. __________consists of independent experts making statements to target buyers.

a) Expert channels

b) Advocate channels

c) Social channels

d) Delivery channels

986. ________consists of neighbors, friends, family and other associates.

a) Expert channels

b) Advocate channels

c) Social channels

d) Delivery channels

987. __________are small groups whose members interact frequently.

a) Buzz

b) Liaison

c) Cliques

d) Dramatization

988. A__________ is a person who connects two or more cliques without belonging to either.

a) Buzz
b) Liaison
c) Cliques
d) Dramatization

989. A __________ is a person who belongs to one clique and is linked to a person in another clique.
a) Buzz
b) Liaison
c) Cliques
d) Bridge

990. ____________involves passing on company developed products, services or information from user to user.
a) Holistic marketing
b) Personnel marketing
c) Societal marketing
d) Viral marketing

991. ____________is a one-time mailing offering.
a) Single stage Campaign
b) Multistage Campaign
c) Multi vehicle Campaign
d) Integrated marketing communications

992. Designing effective advertising campaigns is:
a) Science
b) Arts
c) Both Science and Arts
d) Engineering design

993. In developing a message strategy a developer usually goes through:

a) Two steps
b) Three steps
c) Four steps
d) Five steps

994. ______________ asks consumers to view or listen to a assortment of advertisements.
a) Portfolio tests
b) Laboratory tests
c) On-air tests
d) All the above
995. ___________use equipment to measure physiological reactions.
a) Portfolio tests
b) Laboratory tests
c) On-air tests
d) All the above
996. _________time is the time necessary to prepare the program prior to its launch.
a) Sell in
b) Lag
c) Trail
d) Lead
997. _________method focuses on potential exposure to the brand by assessing the extent of media coverage.
a) Demand side
b) Media side
c) Supply side
d) Both a & c
998. ___________method focuses on reported exposure from consumers.

a) Demand side
b) Media side
c) Supply side
d) Both a & c
999. A workload approach consists of ________steps.
a) Four
b) Five

c) Six

d) Eight

1000. _________has resulted in an ever increasing number of market niches.

a) Market pacification

b) Market demassification

c) Market amplification

d) All the above

# References


Philip Kotler, Gary Armstrong, Veronica Wong & John Saunders, (2008) "**Principles of marketing**" (fifth edition)

Frances Brassington, Stephen Pettitt (2006), "**Principles of Marketing**" (Fourth Edition)

MadhuvantiSathe, Aditi Markale, DhananjayMandlik, Avinash Joshi &AnuradhaKhare (2012), "**Services Management – Call for the Future**".

Nitin Kamat&Chinmay Nitin Kamat, (2017), "**Digital Marketing**".

NishantVacchani& Sanjay Bhayani (2016), "**Basics of E-Marketing**".

S.A. Chunawalla (2016), "**Advertising, Sales and Promotion Management**"

K. Karunakaran (2016), "**Marketing Management (Text and Cases in Indian Context)**".

M. Jayappa, M.S. Iqbal & M. Chandnani (2016), "**Business Marketing**"

Suja R. Nair (2016), "**Consumer Behaviour and Marketing Research**".

Biplab S. Bose (2015), "**Marketing Management**".

S. Banumathy& M. Jayalakshmi (2015), "**Retail Marketing**"

S.A. Sherlekar& R. Krishnamoorthy (2016), "Marketing Management (Concepts and Cases)".

S. Shajahan (2016), "**Services Marketing (Concepts, Practices &**

**Cases)".**

M.N. Mishra (2015), "**Modern Marketing Research**"

Francis Cherunilam (2015), "**International Marketing**"

S.A. Chunawalla (2014), "**Sales and Distribution Management**".

S.M. Jha (2015) "**Services Marketing**"

S.L. Gupta (2014), "**Brand Management (Text and Cases)**".

Suja R. Nair (2014), "**Marketing Research**".

Philip Kotler & Kevin Lane Keller,(2006), "**Marketing Management**" 12th edition.

Philip Kotler, Gary Armstrong (1980), "**Principles of Marketing**".

Philip Kotler (2003) "**Marketing Insights from A to Z: 80 Concepts Every Manager Needs to Know**".

Philip Kotler (2009), "**Marketing Management: A South Asian Perspective**".

Philip Kotler, Kevin Lane Keller (2004), "**A Framework for Marketing Management**"

Philip Kotler&Alexander Chernev (2008),"**Strategic Marketing Management**".

Philip Kotler, Irving Rein (1993) "**Marketing Places**".

Philip Kotler, Gary Armstrong (2012), "**Marketing: An Introduction**".

Philip Kotler (2008), "Principles of Marketing", (12th International Edition).

Philip Kotler (1980), "**Positioning: The Battle for Your Mind**".

Philip Kotler (2004), "**Marketing Management and Marketing Plan**".

Alan Andreessen, Philip Kotler (2003), "**Strategic Marketing for Nonprofit Organizations**".

# ANSWER KEY

| Q. | Ans. | Q. | Ans. | Q. | Ans. | Q. | Ans. |
|---|---|---|---|---|---|---|---|
| 1 | A | 43 | A | 85 | A | 127 | A |
| 2 | D | 44 | C | 86 | B | 128 | B |
| 3 | B | 45 | D | 87 | B | 129 | C |
| 4 | A | 46 | C | 88 | B | 130 | D |
| 5 | B | 47 | A | 89 | A | 131 | A |
| 6 | A | 48 | A | 90 | B | 132 | B |
| 7 | C | 49 | C | 91 | C | 133 | A |
| 8 | A | 50 | B | 92 | A | 134 | B |
| 9 | A | 51 | B | 93 | D | 135 | B |
| 10 | B | 52 | A | 94 | A | 136 | A |
| 11 | B | 53 | C | 95 | C | 137 | D |
| 12 | A | 54 | B | 96 | B | 138 | B |
| 13 | B | 55 | D | 97 | C | 139 | C |
| 14 | A | 56 | C | 98 | A | 140 | A |
| 15 | C | 57 | B | 99 | B | 141 | C |

| | | | | | | | |
|---|---|---|---|---|---|---|---|
| 16 | A | 58 | B | 100 | D | 142 | A |
| 17 | D | 59 | C | 101 | B | 143 | B |
| 18 | D | 60 | A | 102 | B | 144 | C |
| 19 | B | 61 | A | 103 | A | 145 | B |
| 20 | B | 62 | B | 104 | A | 146 | C |
| 21 | D | 63 | D | 105 | B | 147 | B |
| 22 | A | 64 | C | 106 | C | 148 | A |
| 23 | B | 65 | D | 107 | D | 149 | B |
| 24 | C | 66 | A | 108 | A | 150 | C |
| 25 | A | 67 | B | 109 | A | 151 | B |
| 26 | B | 68 | C | 110 | B | 152 | D |
| 27 | C | 69 | D | 111 | C | 153 | A |
| 28 | D | 70 | B | 112 | B | 154 | B |
| 29 | C | 71 | A | 113 | A | 155 | D |
| 30 | A | 72 | A | 114 | B | 156 | A |
| 31 | A | 73 | B | 115 | C | 157 | C |
| 32 | B | 74 | C | 116 | C | 158 | B |
| 33 | C | 75 | B | 117 | B | 159 | A |
| 34 | D | 76 | C | 118 | A | 160 | D |
| 35 | D | 77 | A | 119 | A | 161 | B |
| 36 | B | 78 | B | 120 | D | 162 | A |
| 37 | C | 79 | B | 121 | A | 163 | B |
| 38 | A | 80 | B | 122 | B | 164 | B |

| | | | | | | | |
|---|---|---|---|---|---|---|---|
| 39 | B | 81 | A | 123 | C | 165 | A |
| 40 | C | 82 | B | 124 | C | 166 | C |
| 41 | A | 83 | C | 125 | A | 167 | A |
| 42 | B | 84 | C | 126 | B | 168 | B |
| 169 | C | 214 | B | 259 | D | 304 | C |
| 170 | A | 215 | B | 260 | D | 305 | A |
| 171 | B | 216 | A | 261 | A | 306 | B |
| 172 | B | 217 | C | 262 | A | 307 | C |
| 173 | A | 218 | A | 263 | A | 308 | A |
| 174 | B | 219 | B | 264 | B | 309 | B |
| 175 | D | 220 | C | 265 | C | 310 | C |
| 176 | C | 221 | A | 266 | A | 311 | A |
| 177 | A | 222 | B | 267 | C | 312 | B |
| 178 | A | 223 | A | 268 | C | 313 | B |
| 179 | B | 224 | A | 269 | A | 314 | A |
| 180 | C | 225 | B | 270 | B | 315 | B |
| 181 | D | 226 | C | 271 | B | 316 | A |
| 182 | A | 227 | D | 272 | A | 317 | B |
| 183 | B | 228 | A | 273 | A | 318 | B |
| 184 | C | 229 | B | 274 | C | 319 | B |
| 185 | D | 230 | A | 275 | B | 320 | D |
| 186 | B | 231 | C | 276 | C | 321 | A |
| 187 | A | 232 | C | 277 | A | 322 | A |

| | | | | | | | |
|---|---|---|---|---|---|---|---|
| 188 | C | 233 | B | 278 | B | 323 | B |
| 189 | C | 234 | B | 279 | A | 324 | C |
| 190 | B | 235 | A | 280 | B | 325 | D |
| 191 | A | 236 | C | 281 | C | 326 | C |
| 192 | A | 237 | D | 282 | D | 327 | A |
| 193 | C | 238 | C | 283 | A | 328 | B |
| 194 | C | 239 | A | 284 | B | 329 | A |
| 195 | C | 240 | B | 285 | C | 330 | B |
| 196 | A | 241 | D | 286 | B | 331 | C |
| 197 | B | 242 | A | 287 | A | 332 | D |
| 198 | C | 243 | D | 288 | C | 333 | A |
| 199 | D | 244 | B | 289 | D | 334 | D |
| 200 | C | 245 | D | 290 | A | 335 | C |
| 201 | D | 246 | B | 291 | C | 336 | A |
| 202 | A | 247 | B | 292 | B | 337 | C |
| 203 | B | 248 | D | 293 | C | 338 | B |
| 204 | A | 249 | A | 294 | C | 339 | A |
| 205 | B | 250 | A | 295 | D | 340 | C |
| 206 | C | 251 | A | 296 | B | 341 | C |
| 207 | B | 252 | C | 297 | C | 342 | D |
| 208 | D | 253 | A | 298 | D | 343 | C |
| 209 | D | 254 | B | 299 | C | 344 | A |
| 210 | C | 255 | C | 300 | A | 345 | C |

| 211 | C | 256 | A | 301 | D | 346 | B |
|---|---|---|---|---|---|---|---|
| 212 | A | 257 | B | 302 | A | 347 | B |
| 213 | B | 258 | B | 303 | D | 348 | C |
| 349 | C | 394 | C | 439 | B | 484 | D |
| 350 | A | 395 | D | 440 | A | 485 | D |
| 351 | C | 396 | D | 441 | A | 486 | A |
| 352 | A | 397 | C | 442 | A | 487 | B |
| 353 | B | 398 | D | 443 | A | 488 | C |
| 354 | B | 399 | B | 444 | B | 489 | C |
| 355 | C | 400 | A | 445 | B | 490 | C |
| 356 | D | 401 | C | 446 | B | 491 | A |
| 357 | C | 402 | C | 447 | A | 492 | B |
| 358 | B | 403 | B | 448 | C | 493 | C |
| 359 | A | 404 | A | 449 | B | 494 | B |
| 360 | C | 405 | B | 450 | A | 495 | A |
| 361 | A | 406 | C | 451 | A | 496 | A |
| 362 | D | 407 | D | 452 | B | 497 | B |
| 363 | D | 408 | D | 453 | C | 498 | C |
| 364 | B | 409 | A | 454 | D | 499 | A |
| 365 | D | 410 | B | 455 | A | 500 | A |
| 366 | C | 411 | A | 456 | A | 501 | B |
| 367 | D | 412 | A | 457 | B | 502 | B |
| 368 | B | 413 | B | 458 | C | 503 | C |

| | | | | | | | |
|---|---|---|---|---|---|---|---|
| 369 | C | 414 | C | 459 | D | 504 | A |
| 370 | D | 415 | D | 460 | C | 505 | B |
| 371 | D | 416 | A | 461 | B | 506 | A |
| 372 | A | 417 | B | 462 | A | 507 | D |
| 373 | B | 418 | C | 463 | A | 508 | C |
| 374 | A | 419 | A | 464 | B | 509 | C |
| 375 | B | 420 | A | 465 | C | 510 | A |
| 376 | C | 421 | A | 466 | A | 511 | D |
| 377 | A | 422 | A | 467 | B | 512 | D |
| 378 | B | 423 | B | 468 | C | 513 | C |
| 379 | C | 424 | A | 469 | B | 514 | B |
| 380 | A | 425 | C | 470 | A | 515 | A |
| 381 | A | 426 | A | 471 | C | 516 | B |
| 382 | B | 427 | B | 472 | C | 517 | C |
| 383 | C | 428 | A | 473 | A | 518 | C |
| 384 | D | 429 | D | 474 | B | 519 | B |
| 385 | A | 430 | C | 475 | C | 520 | C |
| 386 | C | 431 | A | 476 | D | 521 | A |
| 387 | D | 432 | B | 477 | D | 522 | A |
| 388 | B | 433 | A | 478 | D | 523 | A |
| 389 | A | 434 | C | 479 | C | 524 | C |
| 390 | B | 435 | C | 480 | D | 525 | D |
| 391 | A | 436 | A | 481 | A | 526 | C |

| 392 | B | 437 | B | 482 | B | 527 | A |
|---|---|---|---|---|---|---|---|
| 393 | D | 438 | A | 483 | C | 528 | B |
| 529 | C | 574 | D | 619 | A | 664 | C |
| 530 | D | 575 | A | 620 | B | 665 | D |
| 531 | A | 576 | B | 621 | C | 666 | A |
| 532 | B | 577 | C | 622 | B | 667 | B |
| 533 | C | 578 | A | 623 | A | 668 | C |
| 534 | D | 579 | B | 624 | D | 669 | D |
| 535 | A | 580 | D | 625 | C | 670 | A |
| 536 | A | 581 | C | 626 | A | 671 | B |
| 537 | B | 582 | C | 627 | B | 672 | C |
| 538 | C | 583 | A | 628 | B | 673 | A |
| 539 | B | 584 | B | 629 | D | 674 | A |
| 540 | D | 585 | D | 630 | A | 675 | A |
| 541 | B | 586 | A | 631 | A | 676 | B |
| 542 | A | 587 | B | 632 | A | 677 | A |
| 543 | C | 588 | C | 633 | C | 678 | B |
| 544 | A | 589 | B | 634 | B | 679 | A |
| 545 | B | 590 | A | 635 | A | 680 | C |
| 546 | C | 591 | D | 636 | D | 681 | D |
| 547 | D | 592 | A | 637 | C | 682 | D |
| 548 | C | 593 | C | 638 | D | 683 | B |
| 549 | B | 594 | B | 639 | D | 684 | A |

| 550 | A | 595 | A | 640 | D | 685 | A |
|---|---|---|---|---|---|---|---|
| 551 | A | 596 | A | 641 | C | 686 | C |
| 552 | D | 597 | C | 642 | A | 687 | C |
| 553 | C | 598 | B | 643 | D | 688 | A |
| 554 | B | 599 | C | 644 | C | 689 | B |
| 555 | D | 600 | A | 645 | D | 690 | C |
| 556 | C | 601 | A | 646 | B | 691 | D |
| 557 | A | 602 | C | 647 | D | 692 | C |
| 558 | A | 603 | D | 648 | D | 693 | A |
| 559 | B | 604 | A | 649 | A | 694 | B |
| 560 | A | 605 | C | 650 | B | 695 | B |
| 561 | A | 606 | B | 651 | A | 696 | C |
| 562 | B | 607 | C | 652 | D | 697 | B |
| 563 | C | 608 | A | 653 | D | 698 | C |
| 564 | B | 609 | B | 654 | B | 699 | D |
| 565 | A | 610 | B | 655 | A | 700 | C |
| 566 | C | 611 | D | 656 | B | 701 | B |
| 567 | D | 612 | D | 657 | C | 702 | C |
| 568 | A | 613 | B | 658 | D | 703 | A |
| 569 | B | 614 | A | 659 | A | 704 | B |
| 570 | B | 615 | A | 660 | B | 705 | C |
| 571 | B | 616 | B | 661 | C | 706 | D |
| 572 | A | 617 | C | 662 | A | 707 | B |

| 573 | B | 618 | D | 663 | B | 708 | A |
|---|---|---|---|---|---|---|---|
| 709 | C | 754 | C | 799 | C | 844 | D |
| 710 | D | 755 | A | 800 | D | 845 | B |
| 711 | B | 756 | C | 801 | A | 846 | B |
| 712 | A | 757 | A | 802 | B | 847 | C |
| 713 | D | 758 | B | 803 | C | 848 | C |
| 714 | A | 759 | C | 804 | D | 849 | C |
| 715 | C | 760 | B | 805 | B | 850 | C |
| 716 | C | 761 | A | 806 | B | 851 | C |
| 717 | B | 762 | B | 807 | B | 852 | A |
| 718 | A | 763 | B | 808 | A | 853 | B |
| 719 | D | 764 | C | 809 | A | 854 | C |
| 720 | B | 765 | C | 810 | A | 855 | D |
| 721 | C | 766 | B | 811 | B | 856 | A |
| 722 | B | 767 | A | 812 | C | 857 | C |
| 723 | D | 768 | D | 813 | D | 858 | B |
| 724 | B | 769 | B | 814 | B | 859 | D |
| 725 | D | 770 | C | 815 | C | 860 | C |
| 726 | A | 771 | B | 816 | D | 861 | A |
| 727 | B | 772 | B | 817 | C | 862 | C |
| 728 | C | 773 | A | 818 | D | 863 | B |
| 729 | D | 774 | B | 819 | B | 864 | A |
| 730 | A | 775 | A | 820 | A | 865 | C |

| | | | | | | | |
|---|---|---|---|---|---|---|---|
| 731 | B | 776 | C | 821 | B | 866 | B |
| 732 | A | 777 | C | 822 | C | 867 | A |
| 733 | B | 778 | C | 823 | A | 868 | B |
| 734 | C | 779 | A | 824 | A | 869 | A |
| 735 | A | 780 | C | 825 | B | 870 | B |
| 736 | B | 781 | B | 826 | A | 871 | C |
| 737 | C | 782 | C | 827 | A | 872 | B |
| 738 | A | 783 | A | 828 | D | 873 | C |
| 739 | B | 784 | C | 829 | A | 874 | D |
| 740 | C | 785 | B | 830 | C | 875 | B |
| 741 | A | 786 | A | 831 | C | 876 | C |
| 742 | B | 787 | B | 832 | A | 877 | D |
| 743 | D | 788 | A | 833 | B | 878 | A |
| 744 | A | 789 | B | 834 | B | 879 | B |
| 745 | C | 790 | B | 835 | A | 880 | D |
| 746 | C | 791 | A | 836 | A | 881 | B |
| 747 | B | 792 | B | 837 | A | 882 | B |
| 748 | A | 793 | C | 838 | D | 883 | A |
| 749 | C | 794 | A | 839 | C | 884 | B |
| 750 | D | 795 | B | 840 | B | 885 | C |
| 751 | C | 796 | C | 841 | B | 886 | C |
| 752 | A | 797 | A | 842 | A | 887 | A |
| 753 | B | 798 | B | 843 | C | 888 | C |

| | | | | | | | |
|---|---|---|---|---|---|---|---|
| 889 | C | 917 | B | 945 | A | 973 | B |
| 890 | B | 918 | D | 946 | B | 974 | A |
| 891 | C | 919 | A | 947 | C | 975 | C |
| 892 | C | 920 | A | 948 | B | 976 | B |
| 893 | A | 921 | A | 949 | B | 977 | C |
| 894 | B | 922 | A | 950 | A | 978 | A |
| 895 | C | 923 | B | 951 | A | 979 | B |
| 896 | A | 924 | D | 952 | C | 980 | A |
| 897 | A | 925 | C | 953 | B | 981 | C |
| 898 | C | 926 | B | 954 | C | 982 | B |
| 899 | B | 927 | D | 955 | B | 983 | C |
| 900 | A | 928 | D | 956 | A | 984 | B |
| 901 | A | 929 | C | 957 | B | 985 | A |
| 902 | A | 930 | D | 958 | A | 986 | C |
| 903 | A | 931 | C | 959 | A | 987 | C |
| 904 | B | 932 | D | 960 | B | 988 | B |
| 905 | C | 933 | A | 961 | C | 989 | D |
| 906 | A | 934 | D | 962 | B | 990 | D |
| 907 | B | 935 | D | 963 | D | 991 | A |
| 908 | A | 936 | C | 964 | B | 992 | C |
| 909 | D | 937 | D | 965 | C | 993 | B |
| 910 | A | 938 | C | 966 | C | 994 | A |
| 911 | B | 939 | B | 967 | B | 995 | B |

|  |  |  |  |  |  |  |  |
|---|---|---|---|---|---|---|---|
| 912 | A | 940 | C | 968 | A | 996 | D |
| 913 | A | 941 | D | 969 | D | 997 | C |
| 914 | A | 942 | A | 970 | C | 998 | A |
| 915 | C | 943 | D | 971 | C | 999 | B |
| 916 | A | 944 | B | 972 | B | 1000 | B |

9 788193 593097

Printed at Repro India Ltd.